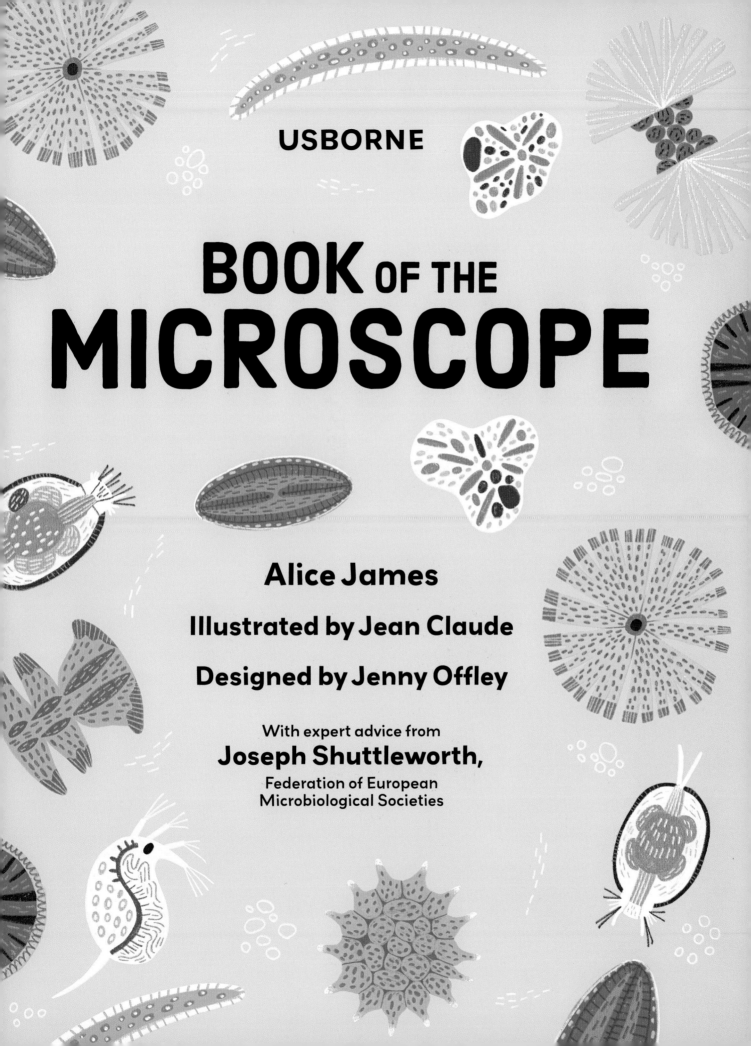

USBORNE

BOOK OF THE
MICROSCOPE

Alice James

Illustrated by Jean Claude

Designed by Jenny Offley

With expert advice from
Joseph Shuttleworth,
Federation of European
Microbiological Societies

Contents

If you have a microscope at home, this is where you can find out the basics of how to use it.

Look out for REAL microscope photos! They have a black outline, like this.

The number means the picture is THAT many times bigger than in real life.

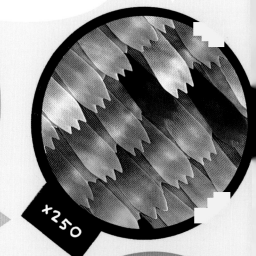

x250

x100

Some pictures are illustrations rather than photos, to make them clearer. Illustrations have a colored outline.

2

When you see one of these symbols, it means there's an experiment for you to do yourself.

This experiment uses a MICROSCOPE.

This one uses a MAGNIFYING GLASS.

Microscopes are very important, and help lots of people to do their jobs. Medical researchers, lab scientists and forensic scientists at crime scenes rely on microscopes every day.

Usborne Quicklinks

For links to websites with videos, photo galleries, games and activities about the microscopic world around us, go to usborne.com/Quicklinks and type in the title of this book. Please follow the internet safety guidelines at Usborne Quicklinks. Children should be supervised online.

Zooming in

A MICROSCOPE allows you to zoom in and discover a whole world of tiny creatures and details. There are two main types. The one below is called an OPTICAL MICROSCOPE. It's the type you might have at home or school.

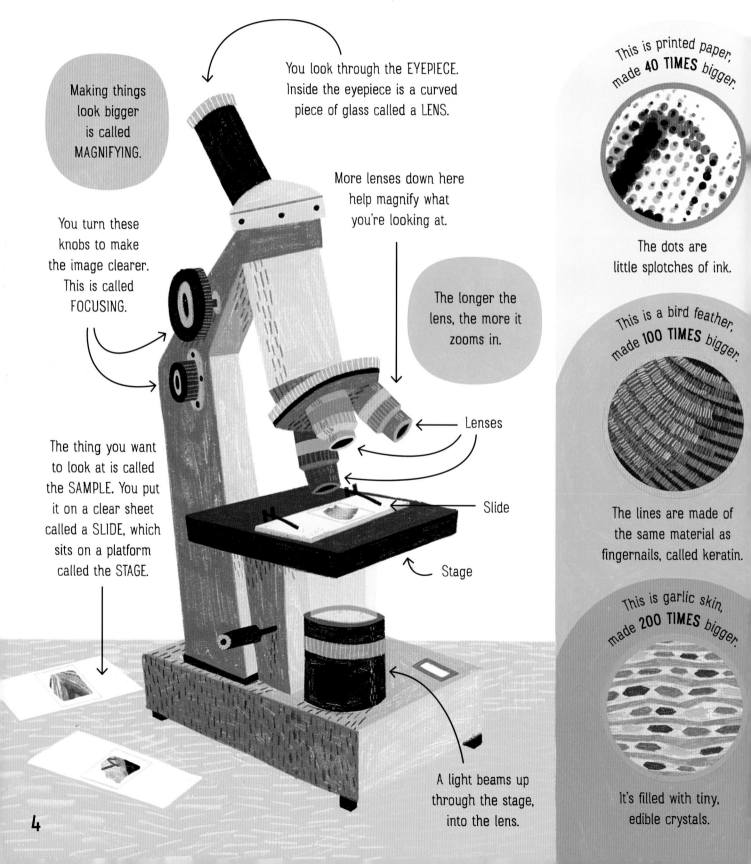

Making things look bigger is called MAGNIFYING.

You look through the EYEPIECE. Inside the eyepiece is a curved piece of glass called a LENS.

More lenses down here help magnify what you're looking at.

You turn these knobs to make the image clearer. This is called FOCUSING.

The longer the lens, the more it zooms in.

The thing you want to look at is called the SAMPLE. You put it on a clear sheet called a SLIDE, which sits on a platform called the STAGE.

Lenses

Slide

Stage

A light beams up through the stage, into the lens.

This is printed paper, made **40 TIMES** bigger.

The dots are little splotches of ink.

This is a bird feather, made **100 TIMES** bigger.

The lines are made of the same material as fingernails, called keratin.

This is garlic skin, made **200 TIMES** bigger.

It's filled with tiny, edible crystals.

There is SO much to discover in the world of the **very, very** small.
With an optical microscope, you can see all sorts of things. Here are just a few.

Tiny creatures in soil

Teeny eight-legged animals, called TARDIGRADES, live in wet soil and other damp places. Find out more about tardigrades on page 38.

We are all miniature living things that you can only see with a microscope!

I'm a tiny FUNGUS.

We are BACTERIA.

I'm another type of bacteria. Follow us all through the book.

Tardigrade
x210

Spreading spores

Livings things called FUNGI reproduce by releasing tiny floating blobs into the air. The blobs are called SPORES.

This is penicillin fungus. The small circles you can see are spores.

The cells that make up living things

ALL living things are made of intricate building blocks called cells. You can read about how people discovered cells on page 14.

Penicillin spores
x100

Grass blade
x145

This photo shows cells joined together in a blade of grass.

Types of fungi include mushrooms, molds and yeast. There's more about them all on pages 24-26.

Zoom in even closer

The most powerful type of microscope is an ELECTRON MICROSCOPE.
Scientists use these in labs, to see things many THOUSANDS
of times bigger than they look in real life.

Electron microscopes use
tiny particles called ELECTRONS
to produce a detailed,
three-dimensional image.

The image on the
right shows the bobbly
surface of a grain of
pollen from a Venus
flytrap plant.

x1,000

Pollen

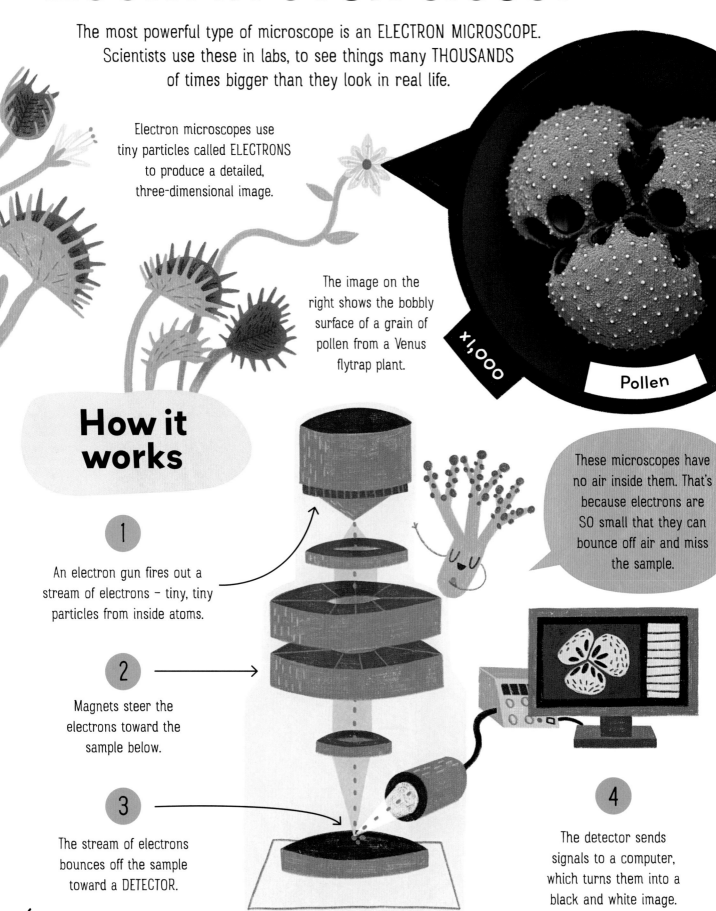

How it works

1

An electron gun fires out a
stream of electrons – tiny, tiny
particles from inside atoms.

These microscopes have
no air inside them. That's
because electrons are
SO small that they can
bounce off air and miss
the sample.

2

Magnets steer the
electrons toward the
sample below.

3

The stream of electrons
bounces off the sample
toward a DETECTOR.

4

The detector sends
signals to a computer,
which turns them into a
black and white image.

After an image has been created, scientists add COLOR to it. The colors aren't really there, but they help you see the features of the image and understand what it shows.

This electron microscope is looking at a virus inside an infected human cell.

What's the difference?

If you look at the same object with an optical and electron microscope, you'll see very different things. Take these two images of a flea...

With an OPTICAL microscope, you can see the flea's basic shape. Can you spot some hairs on its body?

This O tells you it's an OPTICAL microscope image.

x23 O

Flea

Flea

Antenna

Mouth

Through an electron microscope, you see MUCH MORE detail. Look at the flea's hairs this time, and the antennae and mouth.

x42 E

This E tells you it's an ELECTRON microscope image.

Using a microscope

Here's how to set up and use an optical microscope.

1

Take the sample you want to look at and place it on a slide. Put the slide on the stage. Make sure your sample is over the hole in the stage so light can reach it from below.

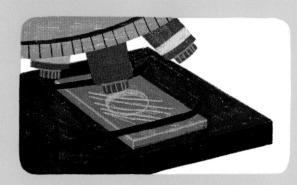

2

Turn on the light below the stage. If your microscope has a mirror instead of a light, set up a lamp and angle the mirror like this.

3

If you have a thick, solid sample, light can't pass through from below. So you might get a better picture by lighting the sample from ABOVE. This is called TOP LIGHTING.

Depending on your microscope, it can be hard to get a good view with top lighting. If you can't see much, try using a magnifying glass instead.

4

Line up one of the lenses above the sample, then look through the eyepiece. Turn the focusing knobs until the image looks sharp and clear.

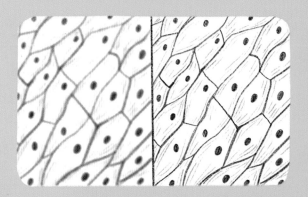

For more microscope tips, and other ways of zooming in, go to pages 60-61.

Around the home

You can use a microscope to discover a lot about things around your home – from what dust is made of to how paper is made. Read on to find out more...

Fabric   x250   O

This image shows fibers of cotton fabric under a microscope.

Fabulous fibers

The threads that make up fabric are made of very thin strands called FIBERS.
Up close, you can make out little differences that reveal what kind of fiber they are.

Here are a few kinds of fiber.
The drawings beneath them show some of their uses.

COTTON from a cotton plant looks like a flattened tube. It often twists, like this.

Clothes   Bedding   Cotton swabs

SYNTHETIC fibers, such as polyester and nylon, are made by machines. They're straight and smooth.

Clothes   Tents   Nets   Carpets

WOOL comes from a sheep and CASHMERE comes from a goat. They both look scaly.

Clothes   Bedding   Carpets

Find some fibers

Very old t-shirt

1 Look around for scraps of fabric or loose threads that you could cut.

2 Separate a few strands of each fabric with tweezers.

3 Put them on a slide. Add a few drops of water too, to keep them in place.

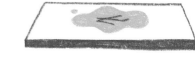

Can you spot the individual fibers WITHIN the thread? Compare what you see to the pictures above - can you work out what type of fabric it is?

If it came from a fabric with a label, you might be able to check if you were right.

LINEN comes from a plant called flax. It has joints that split the fiber into sections.

Aprons

Bedding

Bags

Towels

SILK is produced by silkworm caterpillars. It looks like a hollow tube and sometimes forms a bendy shape.

Clothes

Chair fabric

Bedding

Rugs

Under a microscope, fibers may not look very colorful. But you should be able to see their different textures.

The wonders of weaving

Most fabrics are made by weaving threads together. The properties of a fabric, such as how warm or stretchy it is, depend on the fiber it's made from AND how it's woven.

NYLON can be woven tightly to make warm, waterproof clothing. The gaps between the fibers are so small that water can't get in, and warm air can't escape.

Woven nylon
x35

Loosely woven COTTON is good for cool clothes and bedding. Cotton is light, and gaps in the weave let air pass through.

Woven cotton
x22

x67 E

This swimsuit fabric is woven with tiny ridges. The ridges change the way water flows past the fabric, helping the swimmer to go faster.

Swimsuit fabric

This fabric was inspired by SHARK SKIN, which has ridges too.

Paper and ink

To the human eye, most paper looks completely flat. But a microscope tells a different story. Paper is made of thousands and thousands of fibers, stuck together.

To make most paper, WOOD is shredded into thin fibers...

...mixed with water to make a mushy pulp...

...then dried and pressed to make paper.

Different types of paper are made using fibers from different types of wood and plants, and sometimes by adding specific chemicals to the pulp.

Paper up close

You can often see the fibers more clearly through a microscope if you TEAR the paper and look at the torn edges.

x80 E

Torn paper

This photo shows torn plain paper. But if your paper had things printed on it, look out for dots of ink.

Tear and compare

Find different types of paper to compare under a microscope. **YOU COULD TRY...**

Magazines

Wrapping paper

FUN MAGAZINE

Brown envelopes

Tissue paper

writing paper

MICRO NEWS

Newspapers

Cardboard

① Tear off a small scrap and place it directly on the stage. Light it from below.

② At first it might seem as if you're not looking at anything. But slowly turn the focus knobs, and fibers will appear.

Use the clips to keep the paper flat.

More things to try

Can you see anything that ISN'T a fiber? There might be dust or hair on the paper.

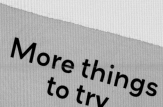

Write on the paper. Pen and pencil might look different. This is because ink pens soak into paper and stain the fibers, while pencil just sits on top.

What does a fold line look like up close?

Cork discovery

In 1665, scientist Robert Hooke was looking at a material called CORK through his microscope, when he made an important discovery. He spotted hundreds of tiny blobs, which he called CELLS.

Here's Hooke's drawing of cork. Each little block is a cell.

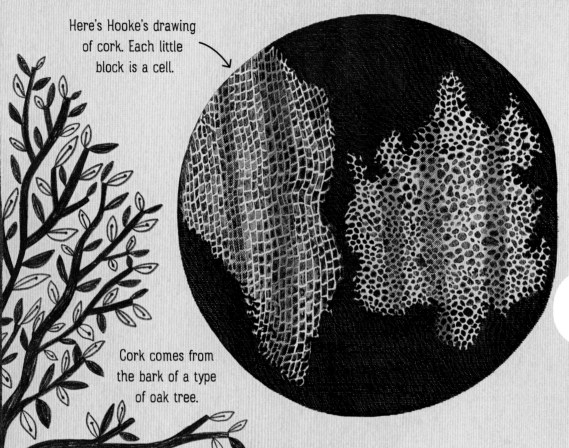

Hooke's discovery was just the start. Over the years as scientists zoomed in FURTHER, they realized cells were clever, complicated structures that are essential to life.

Cork comes from the bark of a type of oak tree.

You can read more about plant cells on pages 28-29.

Find a cell

Like Hooke, you can examine plant cells under a microscope and sketch what you see.

1 One of the easiest places to see cells is in onion skin, as it's very thin. Peel a small sliver of onion skin, and place it on a slide.

2 Light the sample from below. You should be able to see cells lined up in rows.

On the money

If you look really closely at old coins and bills,
they can reveal some surprisingly intricate details.

Inspect a coin

Find a coin and examine it to see what you can spot.
This is easiest using a magnifying glass, but you could try using
a microscope (with lighting from above) as well.

If you have a bill,
take a look at
that too.

Can you see any scratches?
That's a sign the coin has
been used a lot.

Bills are full of tiny
details – dots, marks,
strips and patterns.
These make it much
harder to make
FORGERIES, or
fake bills.

To get the tiniest
details onto coins,
computer-controlled
machines engrave very
precisely into the metal.

These are some of the
anti-forgery details on
a Euro note.

The main
lettering is
called the
LEGEND.

5 Euro note

The legend is
obvious – but
look closer right
around the rim. In
some currencies,
more text appears
when you zoom in.

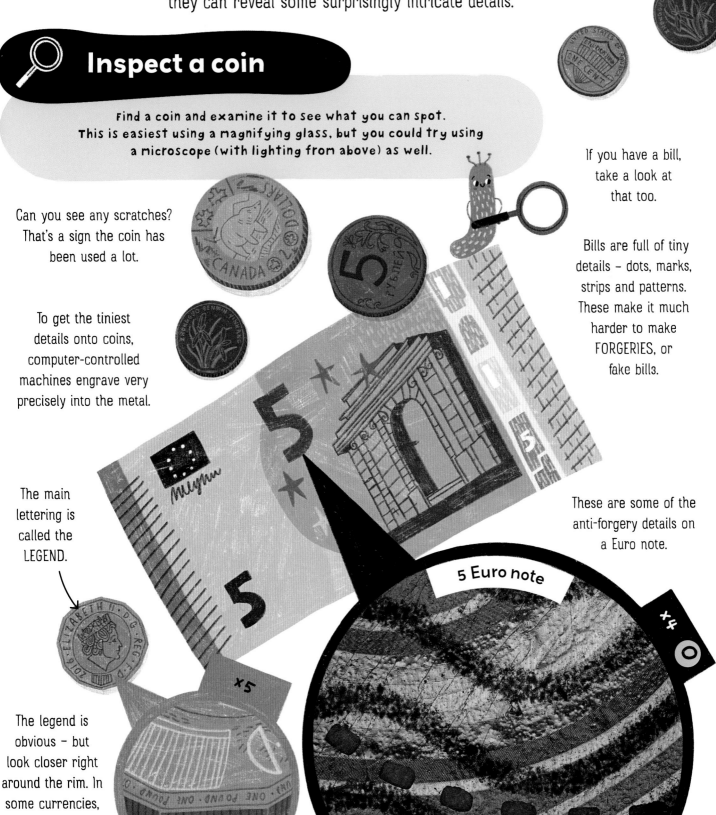

15

Dust detective

The specks of dust that gather around your home contain bits and pieces of ALL SORTS of things...

What's in dust?

Find a dusty surface. Brush some dust onto a slide with your finger. Light it from below. What can you find lurking in it? Look around the page to see some of the things you might find.

Pollen and bits of plants

Hairs

Cotton threads

Human skin

Dust is mostly made of flakes of human skin. Your body is constantly shedding old skin as new skin grows underneath.

Scales from a butterfly wing

Grains of sugar and flour

Insect wings

MUNCH MUNCH

Dust

x50

Dust mite

Dust mites are teeny eight-legged creatures that feed on flakes of skin.

Dust

x260 E

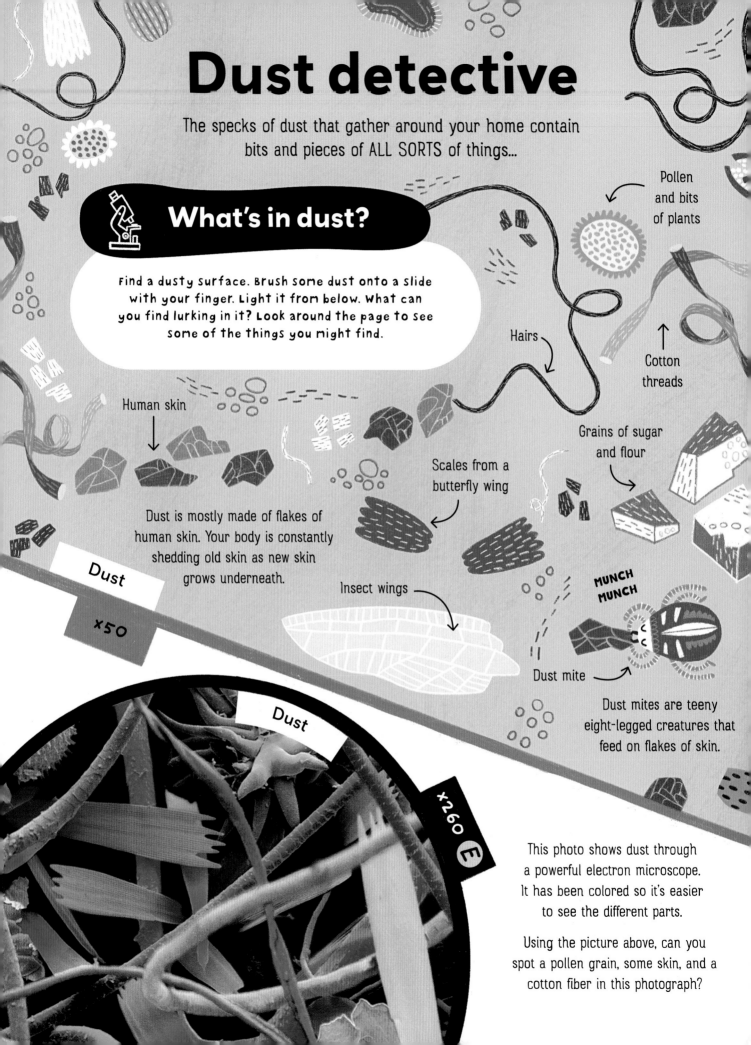

This photo shows dust through a powerful electron microscope. It has been colored so it's easier to see the different parts.

Using the picture above, can you spot a pollen grain, some skin, and a cotton fiber in this photograph?

Holes and bubbles

Take a close look at spongy holes and soapy bubbles in your bathroom.

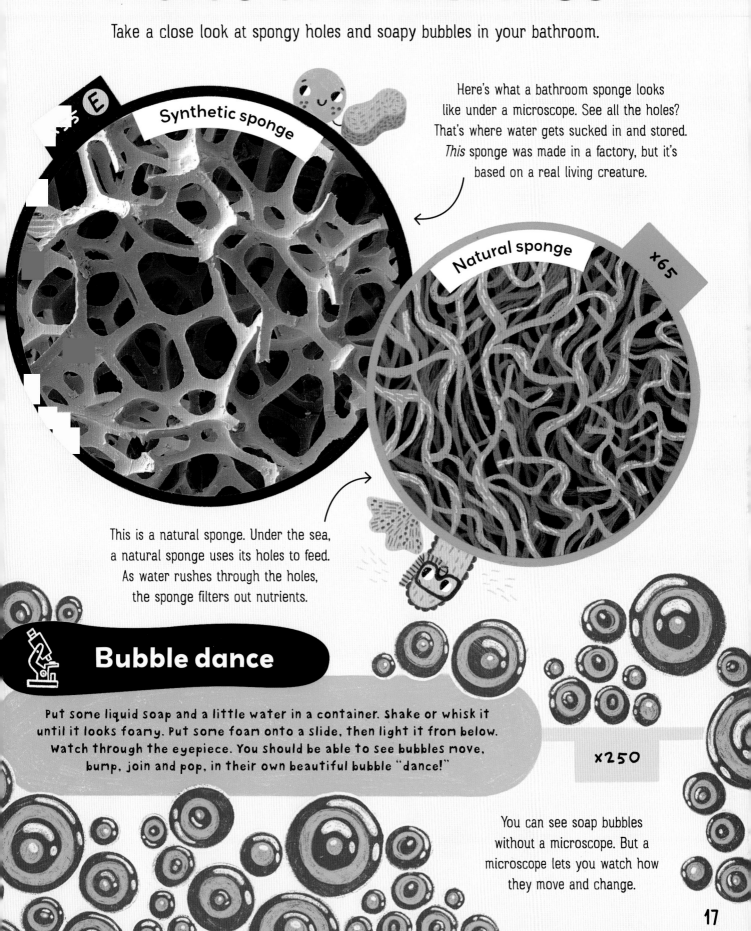

Synthetic sponge

Here's what a bathroom sponge looks like under a microscope. See all the holes? That's where water gets sucked in and stored. *This* sponge was made in a factory, but it's based on a real living creature.

Natural sponge

x65

This is a natural sponge. Under the sea, a natural sponge uses its holes to feed. As water rushes through the holes, the sponge filters out nutrients.

Bubble dance

Put some liquid soap and a little water in a container. Shake or whisk it until it looks foamy. Put some foam onto a slide, then light it from below. Watch through the eyepiece. You should be able to see bubbles move, bump, join and pop, in their own beautiful bubble "dance!"

x250

You can see soap bubbles without a microscope. But a microscope lets you watch how they move and change.

Tiny tech

Modern homes are full of technology, from phones and laptops to cars and washing machines. All these devices contain very small chunks of electronics called CHIPS.

The science of chips

This is the real size of an average chip.

×7

Each chip is packed with miniature wires and switches.

The switches turn ON and OFF as electricity whizzes through them.

The patterns of ONs and OFFs represent information, allowing the chip to "think."

Microchip surface

×250

Zoomed in even further, you can see the lines of miniature wires. These are known as TRACKS.

×100 **E**

Gold connectors

This photo shows how tiny cables connect the chip to the rest of the device.

The cables are made of real gold, which is great at letting electricity buzz through it. Gold is expensive, but chips are so small they only need tiny amounts.

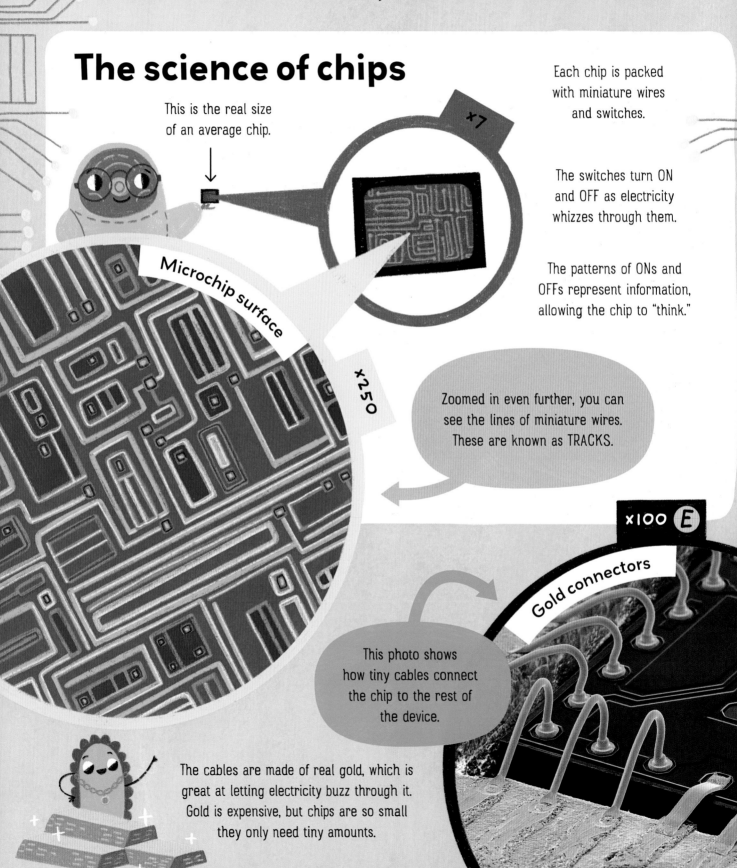

In the kitchen

You might normally be too busy eating to take a very close look at the food in your kitchen. But through a microscope, amazing details appear...

Sugar crystals ×170 O

This shows crystals of sugar that have formed in maple syrup. Color has been added to the photo so you can see the shapes.

Vegetables up close

If you look closely at thin slices of many vegetables, you can spot tiny tubes.
These tubes carry water and other substances around the plant as it grows.

Cucumber

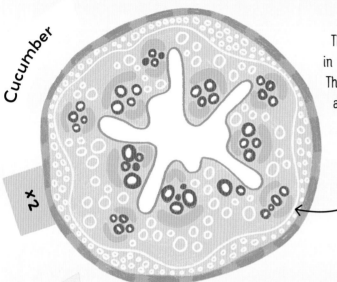

x2

These are the tubes in a slice of cucumber. They're shown in pink and orange so you can see them more clearly.

You may be able to spot the tubes with your eyes alone. But a magnifying glass or microscope will show more detail.

Thin, width-ways slices like these are called CROSS-SECTIONS.

The tubes are called XYLEM (pronounced "z-eye-lem") and PHLOEM (pronounced "flow-em").

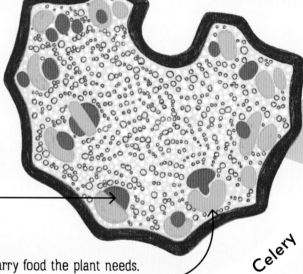

x3

Celery

XYLEM carry water. They're shown in pink.

PHLOEM carry food the plant needs. They're shown in yellow.

Celery staining

You can use food dye to see xylem in action. Here's how.

1 Take half a cup of water, and add a couple of drops of food dye.

2 Cut a stalk of celery and place it in the water. Leave it for a day. You should see dye being pulled up the stalk.

3 Cut a thin cross-section from the bottom of the stalk. Place it on a slide, and light it from below. The xylem will now be stained and easy to spot.

Strong shells

An eggshell may look smooth and simple. But a microscope reveals a surprisingly complicated structure. The shell has to be strong enough to protect a developing chick – but not so strong the chick can't get out.

This is the outside of the shell. It's a thin layer of a crunchy substance called calcium carbonate.

Eggshells are covered in tiny holes, which let air in to reach the chick growing inside. Eggs sold for eating don't have chicks inside, but still have a holey surface.

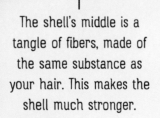

Eggshell

x350 E

The shell's middle is a tangle of fibers, made of the same substance as your hair. This makes the shell much stronger.

This is the super-smooth inside of an eggshell, called a MEMBRANE. It's part of the shell, but can be peeled away separately.

🔍 Spot shell holes

Take a look at a small, flat segment of broken eggshell through a magnifying glass. can you see little holes in the surface?

Eggshell

x12,000 E

21

Kitchen crystals

If you look at salt and sugar up close, a whole range of beautiful shapes appears.
Exactly what type of shape depends on how the salt or sugar was made.

These are grains of granulated sugar. The grains are all very similar sizes because the sugar was processed in a factory.

Sugar

x30

The neat, REGULAR shapes formed by salt and sugar are known as CRYSTALS.

Table salt

x100

These are grains of table salt. Table salt has also been processed – so the crystals are all little cubes.

Sugar

Salt

SEA SALT is made by evaporating sea water. This leaves behind big, flat flakes of salt. The flakes vary in size, and the shapes are less regular.

Other substances called MINERALS are left behind with the salt. They show up as small, colored flecks.

Sea salt

x75

The reason sea salt crystals are more varied is because minerals affect how they form.

Sea salt

Create crystals

1. Using your microscope, first look at SALT OR SUGAR straight out of the package. Pop it on a slide and light it from below. It'll probably look very square and regular.

2. Now create your OWN crystals, which will take on different shapes. Mix two spoons of SALT OR SUGAR into a small amount of warm water.

3. Put a few drops onto a slide. Leave it for a few hours somewhere sunny or warm.

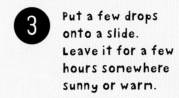

4. The water should evaporate, leaving salt or sugar crystals behind. Light them from below and take a look.

Under the microscope, these crystals should have intricate shapes.

Ice crystals   x75

Freezer ice

Crystals form when things become solid. Sometimes this happens from drying out, sometimes from cooling down. Some of the most incredible crystals in your kitchen can be made in a freezer...

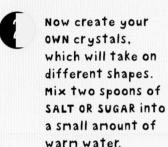

It's difficult to look at ice crystals with a microscope because they melt too quickly. But you can get a good look with a magnifying glass.

Investigate ice

Put a shallow layer of water into a plastic tub or lid and put it in the freezer for a few hours. Take it out, hold it up to the light and look at it with a magnifying glass. Can you see swirly patterns? Those are ice crystals.

Mushrooms and molds

Mushrooms might look like pale lumps at a distance – but through a microscope they are fascinating to explore. Mushrooms are a type of FUNGI, along with molds and yeasts.

Fungi aren't plants or animals, but their own, unique kind of thing.

A fungus can grow in the ground, like a plant, but unlike a plant, it doesn't make its own food. Instead it eats whatever it's growing on.

The mushrooms you buy to eat are actually only PART of a mushroom – a part called the FRUITING BODY.

The thin, papery sections here are called GILLS.

Gills make tiny seeds known as SPORES. The spores drift or fall away and grow into new fungi.

x100

Mushroom gills

Spores

Gills

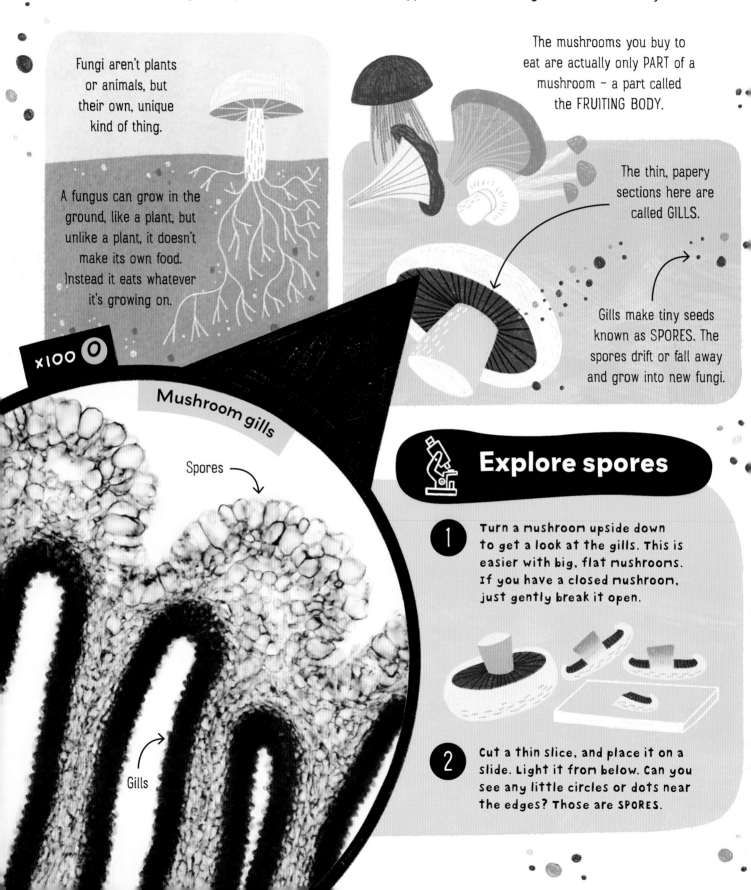

Explore spores

1 Turn a mushroom upside down to get a look at the gills. This is easier with big, flat mushrooms. If you have a closed mushroom, just gently break it open.

2 Cut a thin slice, and place it on a slide. Light it from below. Can you see any little circles or dots near the edges? Those are SPORES.

Yeast

Yeast is a type of fungus that bakers add to dough to make bread rise. It usually comes dried, and looks like a powder. Through a microscope you can see it's actually lots of tiny living things.

There are LOTS of different types of yeast. The one in bread is called baker's yeast.

Yeast releases a gas as it grows, called CARBON DIOXIDE. The gas creates little bubbles and makes the bread rise.

Make yeast bubble

Put a teaspoon of dried baker's yeast and a teaspoon of sugar into some warm water. Wait ten minutes. When the mixture starts to bubble, drop some onto a slide, and light it from below. Can you see individual little circles? They are yeast cells.

DRIED BAKER'S YEAST

Dried yeast is dormant, which means it's sort of asleep. Adding water and waiting ten minutes gives it time to wake up.

Blue cheese

The blue or green streaks in blue cheeses are actually another type of fungus, called MOLD.

The blue blobs in this photo are mold spores. Cheesemakers add this type of mold on purpose, to give their cheese an extra taste.

Spores and the mold that grows from them give the cheese a distinctive flavor...

...and a strong smell!

x650 Ⓔ
Blue cheese

Moldy bread

You might think moldy food is disgusting, but up close it can look amazing. Looking closely at mold is a great way to spot the different parts of a fungus.

If you have asthma or allergies, leave the bread inside the bag.

Grow mold

While you're looking, compare it to the picture below. Can you see any of the labeled parts?

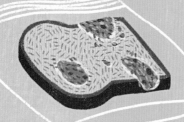
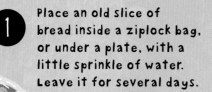

1 Place an old slice of bread inside a ziplock bag, or under a plate, with a little sprinkle of water. Leave it for several days.

2 When you can see some mold starting to form, take it out and carefully look at it with a magnifying glass.

! Don't eat the moldy bread, and wash your hands well after touching it.

Mold on bread `x4`

This is mold that has been growing on bread for seven days.

The dark blobs are SPORE-CARRIERS packed full of little spores to help the mold spread.

The white hair-like strands are called FILAMENTS. More grow every day.

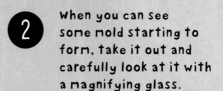

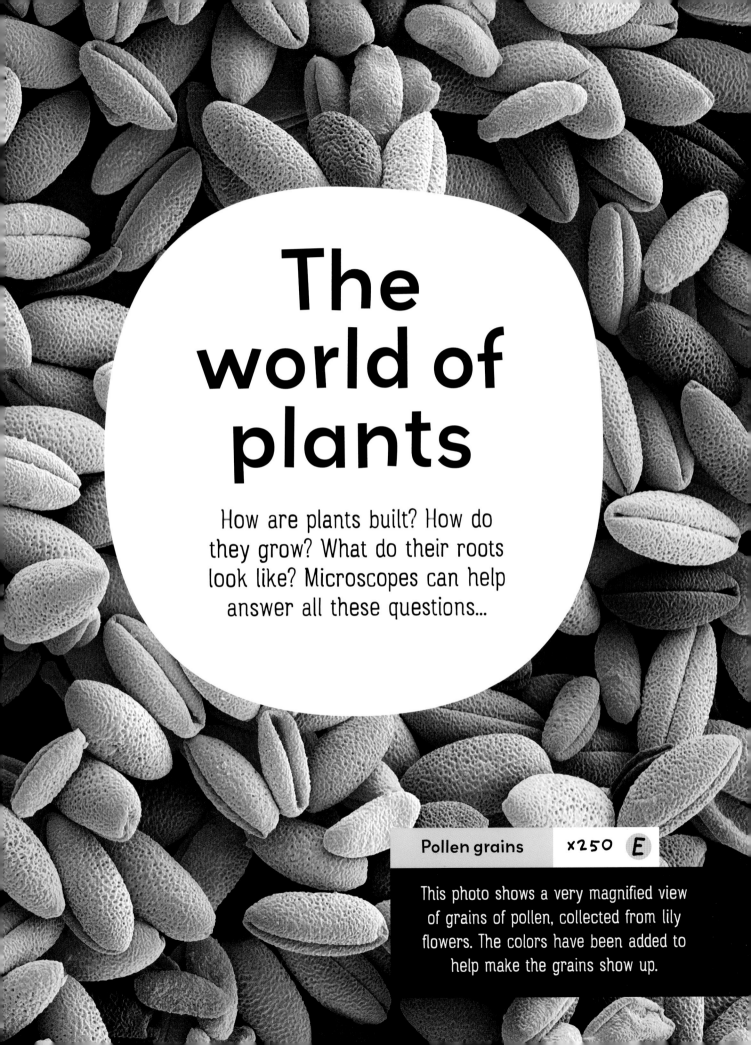

The world of plants

How are plants built? How do they grow? What do their roots look like? Microscopes can help answer all these questions...

Pollen grains   x250   E

This photo shows a very magnified view of grains of pollen, collected from lily flowers. The colors have been added to help make the grains show up.

How are plants built?

Microscopes help us peek INSIDE plants, at the building blocks
that make them up. These building blocks are called CELLS.

Green, green moss

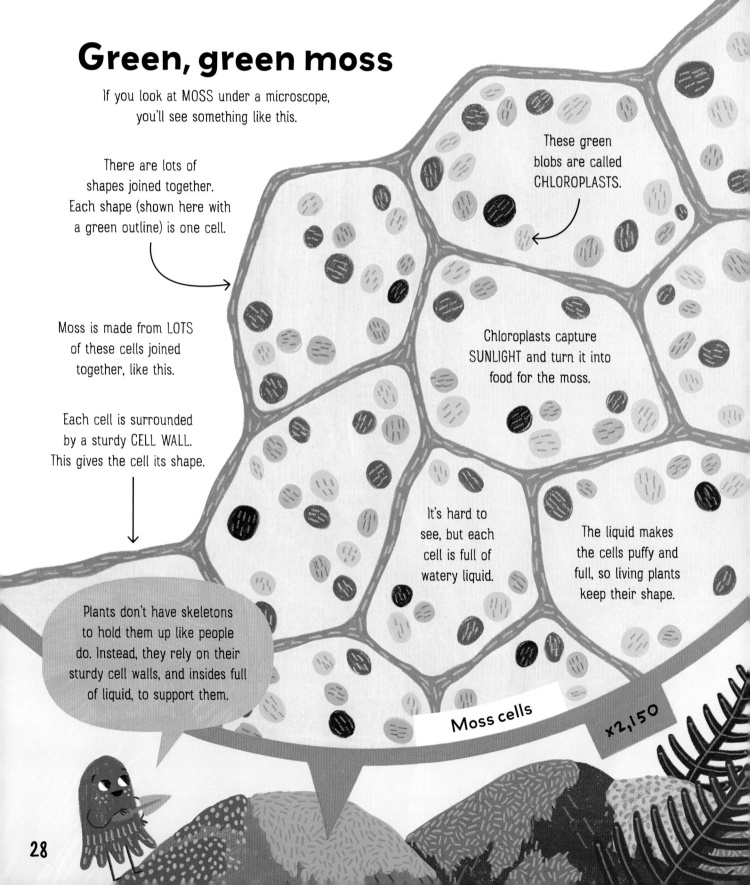

If you look at MOSS under a microscope,
you'll see something like this.

There are lots of
shapes joined together.
Each shape (shown here with
a green outline) is one cell.

Moss is made from LOTS
of these cells joined
together, like this.

Each cell is surrounded
by a sturdy CELL WALL.
This gives the cell its shape.

These green
blobs are called
CHLOROPLASTS.

Chloroplasts capture
SUNLIGHT and turn it into
food for the moss.

It's hard to
see, but each
cell is full of
watery liquid.

The liquid makes
the cells puffy and
full, so living plants
keep their shape.

Plants don't have skeletons
to hold them up like people
do. Instead, they rely on their
sturdy cell walls, and insides full
of liquid, to support them.

Moss cells

x2,150

Find moss cells

1 Moss is green and spongy. It likes growing in dark, shady places. If you can find some growing, pick a few small pieces.

2 Take one piece and place it on a slide. Add a drop of water.

3 Shine your light through it from below and take a look. It should appear very GREEN. That's the chloroplasts. If you zoom all the way in, can you make out any cells?

A cell's brain

Below, you can see ONION SKIN under a microscope.

This sample was taken from a red onion, which is naturally reddish purple in color.

This dark dot in each cell is called the NUCLEUS. It's like the cell's brain. It stores all the instructions that tell the cell what to do.

Onion skin has thin layers, so it's easy to see the cell structure.

You can look at onion skin yourself. Turn back to page 14 for instructions.

Onion skin cells DON'T have any green chloroplasts, because they grow under the ground where there's no sunlight. Their food comes from the green leaves that grow above the ground.

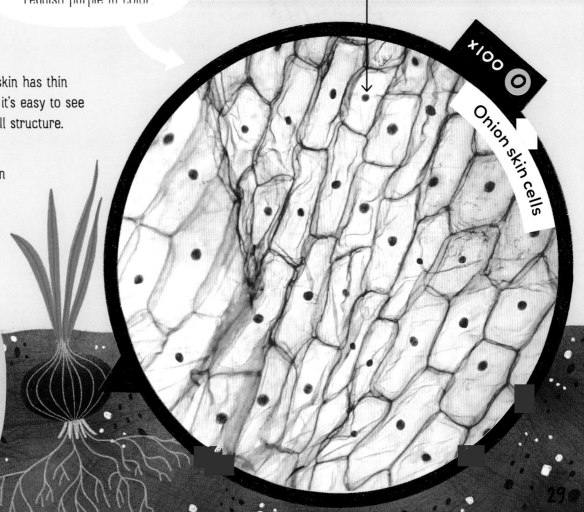

x100

Onion skin cells

29

Petal patterns

To the naked eye, flower petals look smooth and silky,
but zoomed in, a bumpy texture appears.

The cells of a petal are packed full of color. The bright colors
encourage bees, birds and beetles to come closer
and spread POLLEN to help make new plants.

As a petal grows, its cells form
lots of little bumps. Each bump is
coated in a waxy substance, which
makes the petal waterproof and
gives the petal its shiny sheen.

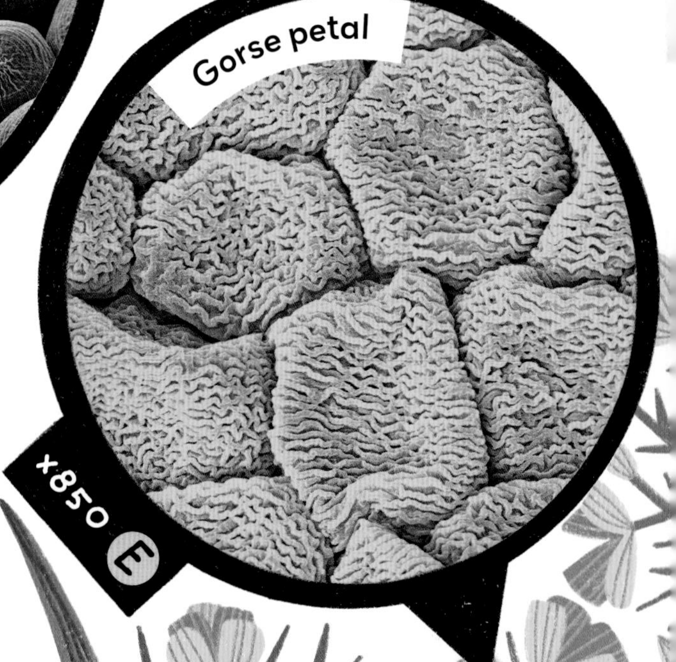

x550 E

Foxglove petal

Gorse petal

x850 E

Find petal textures

Tear off a small piece of petal - the thinner it is, the better.
Pop it on a slide. Light it from below. Can you see any lumps
and bumps? Those are the petal's cells.

Pollen, pollen everywhere

Flowers grow a powder called POLLEN. When pollen from one plant reaches another, it helps create SEEDS.

A powerful microscope reveals the shape of individual pollens grains. The SHAPE of a grain tells you how it travels from plant to plant.

ROUND pollen falls or is blown on the breeze.

SPIKY pollen sticks to insects' bodies and is carried as they move.

These colors have been added to help you see the different shapes more clearly.

x1,000 E

Pollen grains

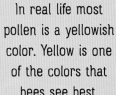

See pollen shapes

1 Find a flower you can pick. Dandelion flowers work well.

2 Tap the flower over a microscope slide.

OR you could take your slide to the flower without picking it.

3 VERY gently add a drop of water (using a dropper works best). Light the slide from below and take a look. Can you spot any grains of pollen floating in the water?

This is pollen under an optical microscope.

In real life most pollen is a yellowish color. Yellow is one of the colors that bees see best.

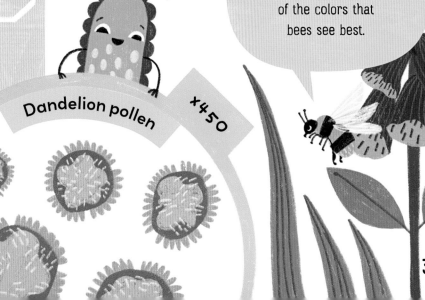

Dandelion pollen   x450

Breathing leaves

The undersides of leaves are covered in TINY holes that let air through.
The holes work like little mouths, letting the plant breathe.

The holes let IN gases that the plant needs,
and let OUT gases it has finished with.

The holes are controlled by GUARD cells. The guards are in charge of OPENING and CLOSING the holes.

OPEN!

Underside of a leaf

x700

The green dots are chloroplasts.

It's not just leaves that have these holes – petals do too. This is what they look like using a powerful electron microscope.

x550 E

Underside of an orchid petal

🔬 Peel a leaf

YOU WILL NEED

A soft leaf (not shiny or waxy)

A piece of clear tape

Clear nail polish

1. Paint a thin layer of nail polish over part of the UNDERSIDE of your leaf. Wait for it to dry.

2. Push a piece of tape onto the dry polish. Lift it off gently. This peels away a THIN section of the underside.

3. Press the tape onto a slide and light it from below. Use your highest magnification and look for the little holes.

Thirsty roots

Under a microscope, roots look surprisingly hairy. These hairs have a very important job – helping the plant to soak up water.

Grow roots

This experiment takes a few days, but you'll get to investigate real living roots.

YOU WILL NEED

cardboard tube   Soil   Water   Seeds, for example mustard or cress seeds

1 Put your tube on an old plate and fill it with soil. Moisten with some water.

2 Drop a couple of seeds on top of the soil. Leave them for a few days.

3 The seeds will burst and sprout little seedlings.

4 Very, very gently pull one seedling out. Try not to break the roots.

5 Put the seedling on a slide. Add a drop of water and light it from below. Can you see little root hairs?

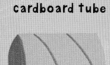

This photo shows the hairs on a root.

Hairy root

x150

Each tiny hair sucks water out of the soil, straight into the root.

Once inside the plant, water moves through tubes, which take it where it's needed.

Growing in water

Have you ever wondered what makes some ponds green and slimy? If you put a drop of pond water under a microscope, you'll see the green comes from lots of tiny living things called ALGAE.

Algae are a little like plants because they are green and make their own food. BUT they don't grow roots, stems or leaves like plants do.

x500

Some types of algae have neat, REGULAR shapes. They are known as DIATOMS.

There are over 10,000 types of diatoms!

What's in the pond?

1 Find a pond where you can collect a little bit of water in a clean jar. Take some from the SURFACE where it appears green.

!

Be careful around the pond, and wash your hands after you touch the water.

2 Take the water home and let it settle. Any mud or sludge will drop to the bottom, but the algae will remain floating.

3 Use a dropper or a spoon to put a few drops of the water gently onto a slide.

4 Light the sample from below and take a look. The rest of this page shows some of the things you might see.

Green algae

This type of algae is so green, it is known as GREEN ALGAE.

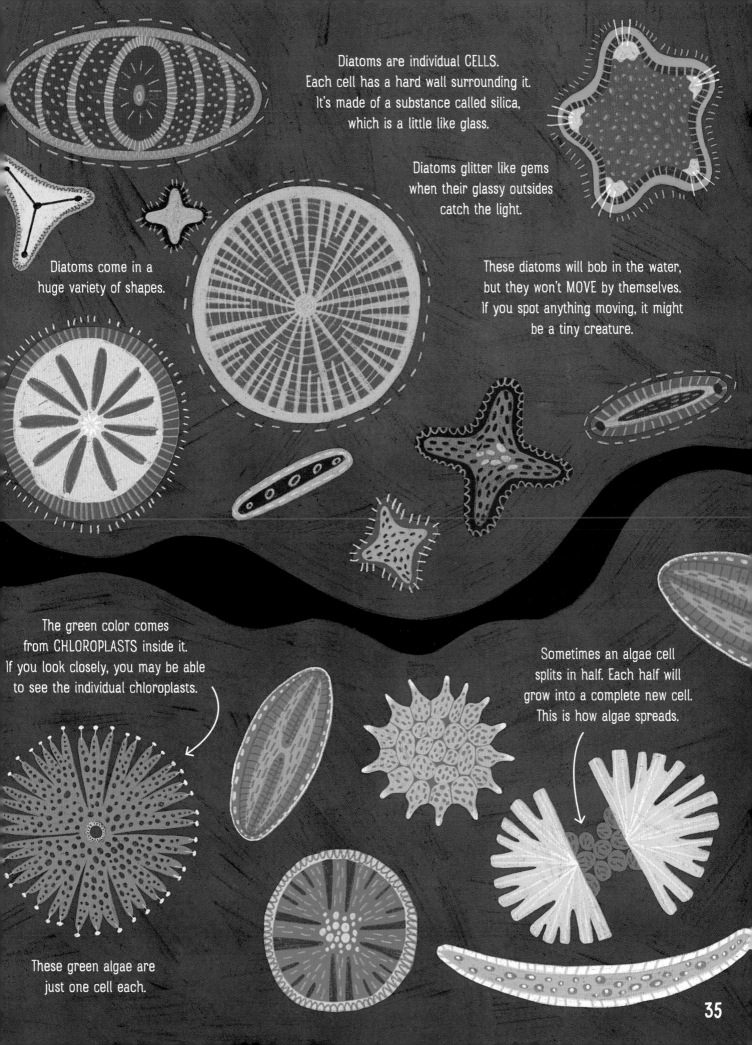

Diatoms are individual CELLS.
Each cell has a hard wall surrounding it.
It's made of a substance called silica,
which is a little like glass.

Diatoms glitter like gems
when their glassy outsides
catch the light.

Diatoms come in a
huge variety of shapes.

These diatoms will bob in the water,
but they won't MOVE by themselves.
If you spot anything moving, it might
be a tiny creature.

The green color comes
from CHLOROPLASTS inside it.
If you look closely, you may be able
to see the individual chloroplasts.

Sometimes an algae cell
splits in half. Each half will
grow into a complete new cell.
This is how algae spreads.

These green algae are
just one cell each.

Prickles and hairs

Through a microscope or magnifying glass, the surface of a soft leaf can suddenly appear furry, rough and bristly, or even spiky.

Hairs on leaves have a range of jobs.

The hairs on this flannelbush leaf protect it from heat and wind. This makes the leaf less likely to dry out and shrivel up.

Flannelbush leaf hairs

x190

How hairy?

Look at a range of leaves with a magnifying glass. These work well:

Sage leaf

Geranium leaf

Lamb's ear leaf

Mint leaf

Can you see any hairs? Are the hairs thick and furry, or are there just a few soft ones? Do any look spiky or sharp?

The hairs on a nettle leaf can give you a painful, itchy sting. This helps to protect the leaf from being eaten or trampled.

The itchy substance is stored at the base of the hair.

x40

Nettle stings

! If you want to look at a stinging nettle, take care not to touch it!

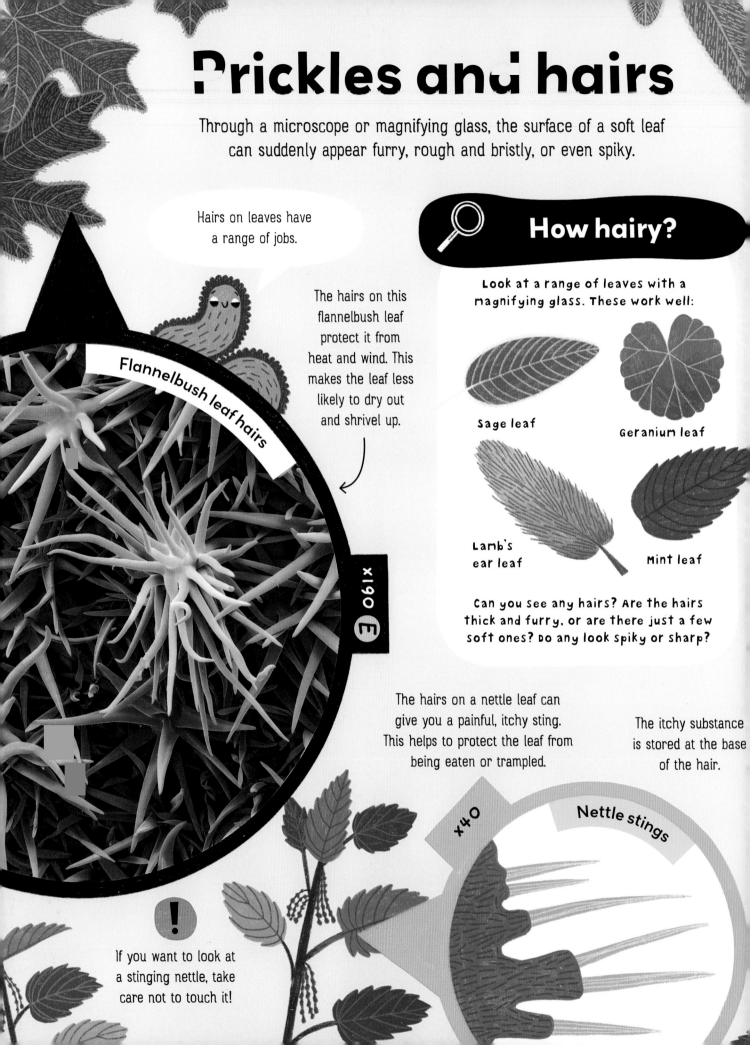

The world of animals

The world is full of teeny, tiny creatures, scuttling and swimming around. Look through a microscope and you can see their hairy bodies, delicate wings and chomping teeth...

Moth wing   x2,500   *E*

This is a photo of the scales on the wing of a moth. The beautiful colors come from tiny ridges on the scales.

Garden minibeasts

Get up close and discover some of the tiniest residents of your backyard or local park.

In the soil

Soil is an ideal home for all sorts of bugs, worms and creepy crawlies.

Worm

This is a SPRINGTAIL. Look through your magnifying glass. You might spot one hopping and jumping.

Centipede

Beetle

🔍 What's in the ground?

Turn over a stone or small log in your garden or a park. Can you see any scuttling beetles or squirming worms?

Now use your magnifying glass to take a closer look. Do any of the other creatures on this page appear?

This is a SOIL MITE. It looks very pale, and moves by crawling around.

Try not to make too much noise, and take your time.

In damp corners

Some of the most amazing minibeasts live in wet places, such as soggy moss, soil or damp flowers.

They are teeny eight-legged TARDIGRADES, also sometimes called moss piglets, because you often find them in moss and they look a little like piglets.

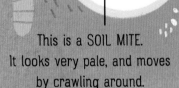

Tardigrade
x550 E

Tardigrades are too small to see without a microscope.

🔬 Find tardigrades

Collect some soft moss. Put it in a pot of water for a day - this wakes up any tardigrades. Spread a few strands of moss on a slide.

Light it from below and look through your microscope. Can you see any small, stubby tardigrades?

On plants

Tiny little bugs called aphids live on plant stems and leaves.

Aphids have a mouth like a little pointy tube. They stick the tube into leaves or stems and SUCK out the plant's sap, as if drinking with a straw.

x30 E

Aphid

Spot an aphid

Take a look on stems or the underside of leaves. Can you see any small green or black bugs? You often find them in big groups.

In the water

Water in a pond or even a puddle can be a perfect place for tiny swimming creatures to live.

x100

Look for pond life

Take a sample of pond water. Put a drop on a slide, and light it from below. Sit back and watch for a few minutes. Can you see things wiggling, swimming and moving?

I'm a WATERFLEA. Can you see my tiny, wafting antennae?

I am a ROTIFER. My mouth is surrounded by a swirl of hairs, which sweep food into my mouth.

I'm an AMOEBA. I'm just a single cell – and I look like a wobbly blob!

A closer look at bugs

If you come across a dead bug, you could look at it under your microscope.

 Investigate fly legs

If your microscope set came with coverslips, use them too. If not, just let the sample dry before you look at it.

YOU WILL NEED

A dead fly (You could try looking for one under a spider's web.)

Clear nail polish

Tweezers

Coverslip

Two slides

1 First, place a drop of nail polish on a slide. This will hold the sample in place.

3 With the tweezers, transfer the leg onto one of the slides. Slowly place the coverslip on top.

2 Using tweezers, very carefully pluck off a LEG. Try to be gentle, but don't worry if some bits break off.

4 Light it from below. What can you see?

!

Wash your hands once you have finished.

House fly leg

x20

All insects have legs that are split into SECTIONS like this.

The hairs help insects sense the world around them AND help them grip onto things.

Look at a wing

Now prepare a dead fly's wing the same way. Light it from below. Can you see the lines of veins through the wing? Or if it's a butterfly wing, can you see any scales?

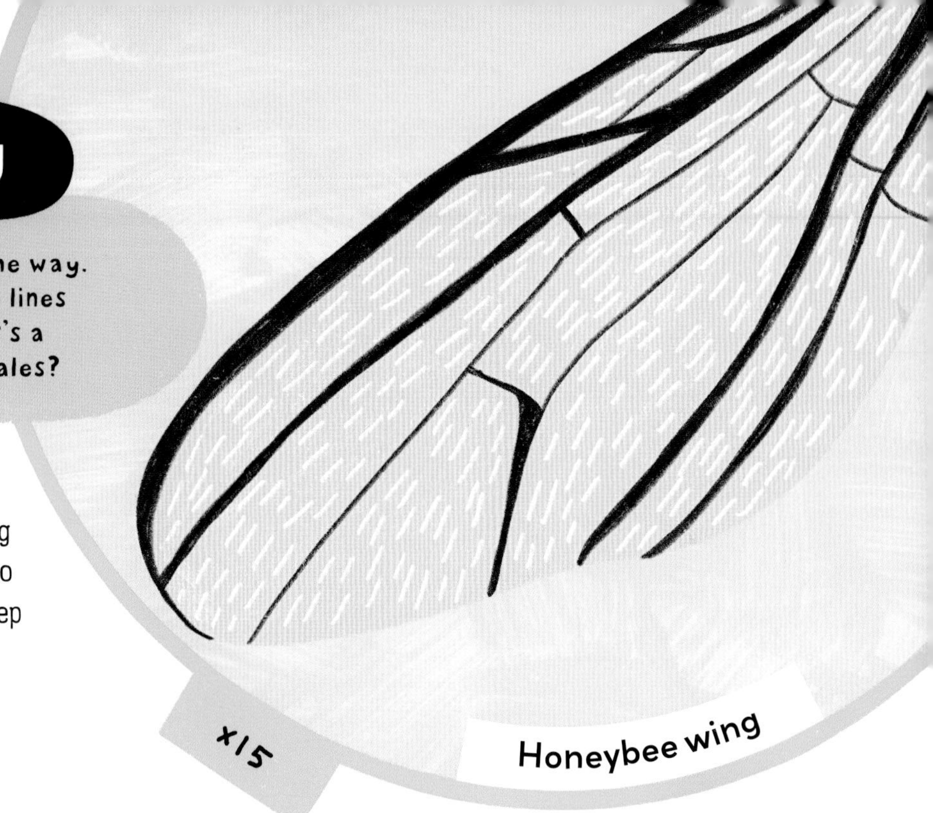

Veins help make the wing STRONGER. Wings need to be light and strong to keep insects up in the air.

x15

Honeybee wing

x475 **E**

Butterfly wing

Butterfly wings are covered in tiny scales.

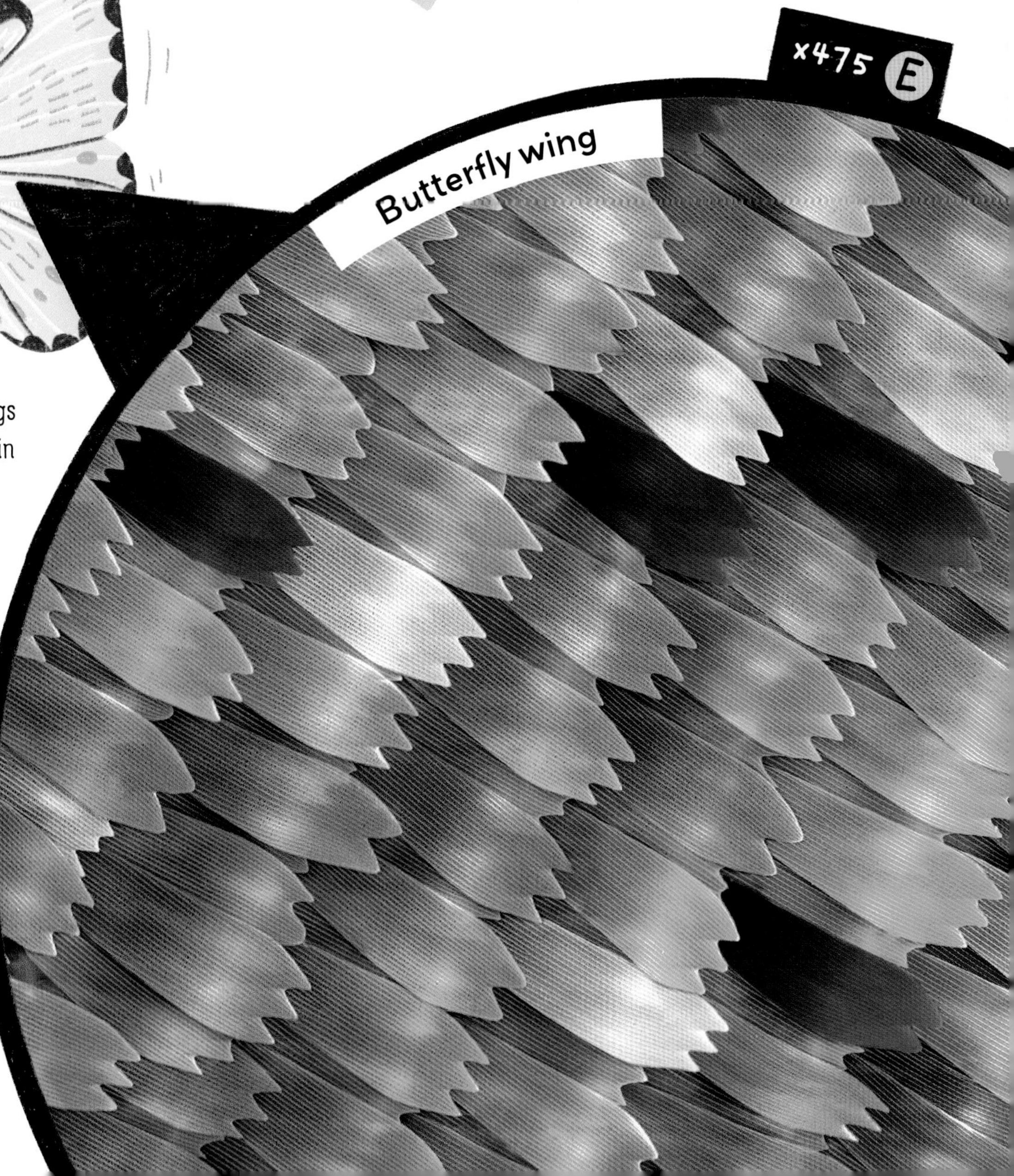

As sunlight shines on the scales, it bounces off and around in all directions. This gives the butterfly its beautiful colors and sheen.

If you find more than one dead bug, you could compare their legs and wings.

Amazing animals

Microscopes aren't only handy for looking at tiny creatures.
Bigger animals have all sorts of features and details that scientists can
only see by zooming in with a powerful electron microscope.

The feet of geckos are covered in tiny hairs,
and each hair ends in a tuft of even TINIER hairs.

The hairs help geckos STICK to
things as they climb. They can
even walk across ceilings.

Gecko foot

x14,000

x40 E

x5,000

These are scales on the skin of a salmon.
All the paler blue lines are RIDGES.

The ridges help the salmon swim
through the water more quickly.

Salmon scales

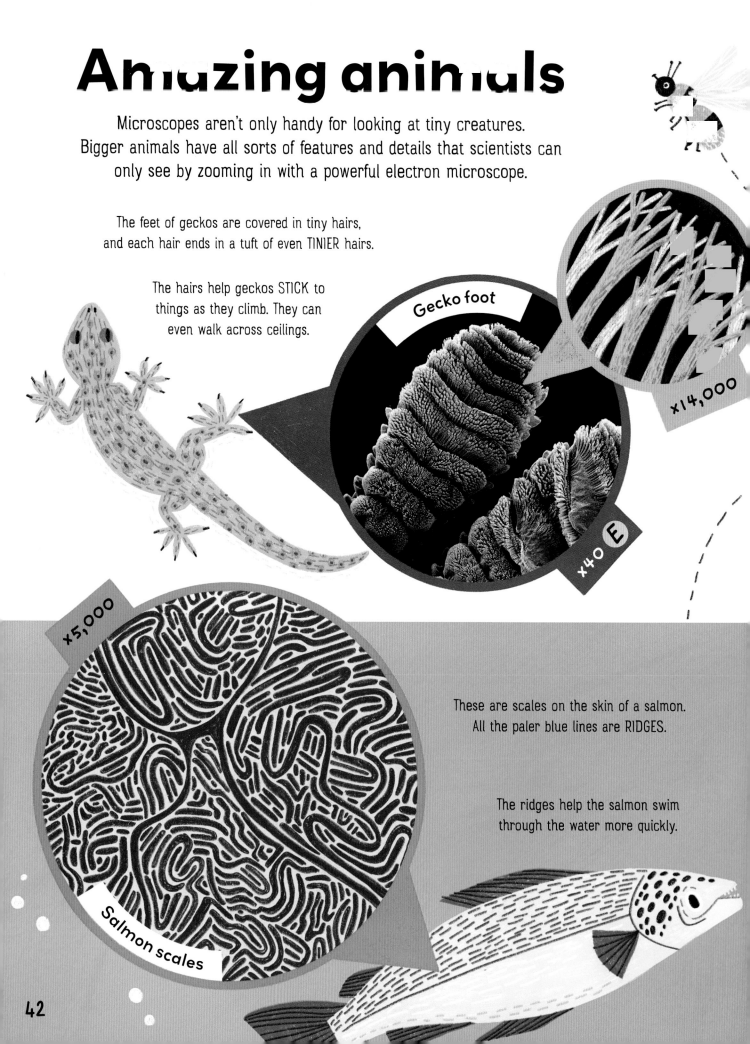

x55 E

Butterfly tongue

This photo shows the curled tongue of a butterfly. When the butterfly uncurls it, it can reach a long way. So the butterfly can slurp up juicy nectar from deep inside a flower.

The eyes of honeybees are covered in little hairs.

The hairs catch pollen and stop it from sticking straight to the eyes. Each hair can pick up a single grain of pollen.

BZZZ

Bee eye

x30

Shark skin is covered in scales that look like spikes. But they're so small that, if you touched the skin, it would just feel slightly rough – like sandpaper.

The spiky shapes cut through the water and help the shark swim faster.

x80 E

Shark skin

This scaly skin inspired engineers to create a new swimwear fabric. There's a photo of it on page 11.

43

Feathers

Birds' feathers are a feat of natural engineering. Looking with a microscope reveals the many parts that make up each feather, and how they work together to do their job.

WING feathers need to be strong and light, to help the bird fly.

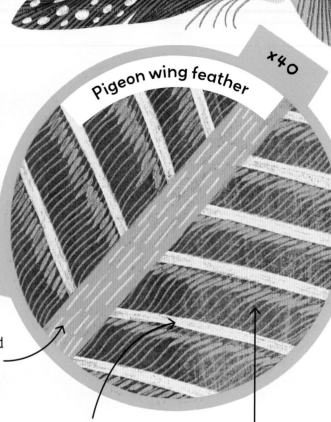

Pigeon wing feather **x40**

This middle part is like the feather's backbone. It's called the SHAFT. It's strong but hollow, which keeps it light.

These lines fanning out from the middle are called BARBS.

The barbs are covered in hundreds of smaller bits called BARBULES. They hook together to make a smooth surface.

Penguin down feathers **x75** Ⓔ

DOWN feathers sit under a bird's outer feathers. They make up a soft, fluffy layer to keep birds warm.

Down feathers are more flexible, and have lots of space between the barbules. This traps air and keeps the bird warm.

See if you can find a feather to look at. You might find one outside, or you could buy one from a craft shop.

Look at a feather

You don't need a slide - just place your feather on the stage and light from below. Can you see the backbone of the feather? Do the barbs look rigid or fluffy?

! If you pick up a feather from outside, wash your hands well afterwards.

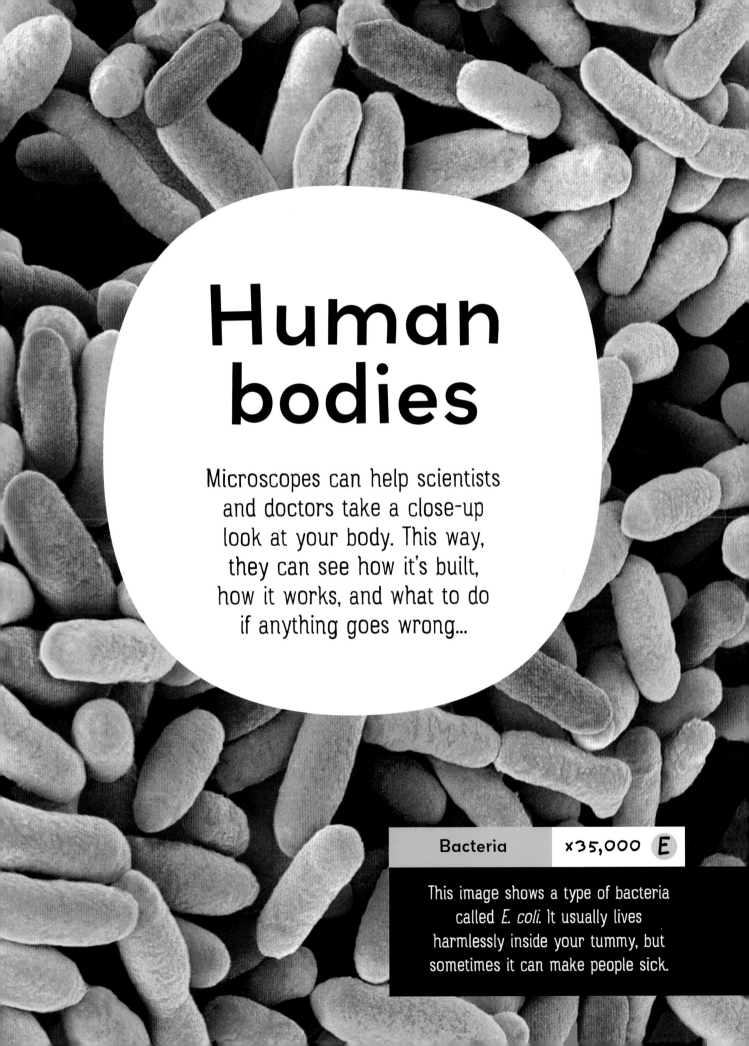

Human bodies

Microscopes can help scientists and doctors take a close-up look at your body. This way, they can see how it's built, how it works, and what to do if anything goes wrong...

Bacteria   ×35,000   E

This image shows a type of bacteria called *E. coli*. It usually lives harmlessly inside your tummy, but sometimes it can make people sick.

Your hair

Your head and body are covered in hairs. A microscope reveals the details of how each strand of hair grows.

x150

Follicles on a scalp

The OUTSIDE of each hair is covered in tiny SCALES.

x200

Your hair grows from tiny holes in your skin called FOLLICLES.

Animal hairs can have scales too. Experts can even tell what TYPE of animal it is by the patterns made by the scales on their hairs.

The purple circles are follicles.

The little red circles are the growing hairs.

The blue parts are skin.

You have follicles all over your skin, EXCEPT for the palms of your hands and soles of your feet.

 Look for a follicle

Use a magnifying glass to look very closely at your arm. Find a hair and look at its base. THAT is a FOLLICLE.

Your cells

Inside your body, you have millions and millions of CELLS. There are around 200 TYPES. Each type has a different job and looks a little different...

Your body is covered with skin cells. Scientists call them EPITHELIAL cells.

These ones have been stained blue to help them show up.

Each cell has a NUCLEUS, which shows up as a dark dot. This is the "brain" of the cell.

Cheek skin cells

x350

Swab your cheek

You can look at your own cheek skin cells using a cotton swab.

1 Rub a clean cotton swab against the inside of your cheek. This collects cheek cells.

2 Gently rub the cotton swab onto a microscope slide.

3 Light the sample from below and take a look. Can you spot wide, flat shapes? Those are your cheek cells.

Other cells
Different body cells have different shapes, depending on what they do.

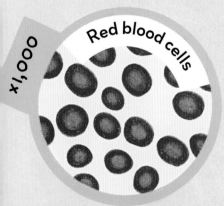

x1,000

Red blood cells

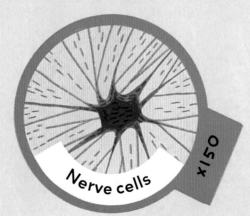

Nerve cells

x150

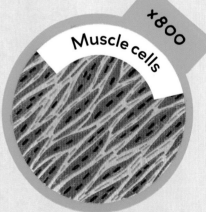

x800

Muscle cells

Red blood cells transport oxygen gas around your body. They look like little, flattened discs.

Nerve cells carry messages around your body. They are long and spindly. This picture shows lots of nerve cells overlapping.

Muscle cells make you move. They are tightly packed and stretchy, so that they can change shape.

47

Inside a brain

Your brain is full of NERVE CELLS, sending messages back and forth as you think.
Using very powerful microscopes and stains that glow in the dark,
scientists in medical labs can see how the cells are packed together.

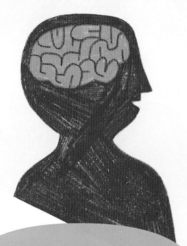

Your brain contains
over 80 BILLION
nerve cells.

This photo shows just
a small section of one
part of a brain.

Each pink dot is a nerve
cell's NUCLEUS.

Each blue or green line is the
main part of a nerve cell.

Studying brains with a
microscope helps scientists
understand how healthy
brains develop and work...

...and how to work out
when something's not
quite right.

The picture below is a close-up of just
one nerve cell. It's from someone with
a disease called Alzheimer's, which can
make people forgetful and confused.

The big blue circle is the nucleus.
The straight blue lines are what brain
scientists call a TANGLE of protein. The tangle
stops the cell from working properly.

Without microscopes,
finding out things
like this would be
impossible.

Damaged nerve cell

x1,000

x650

Nerve cells in the brain

48

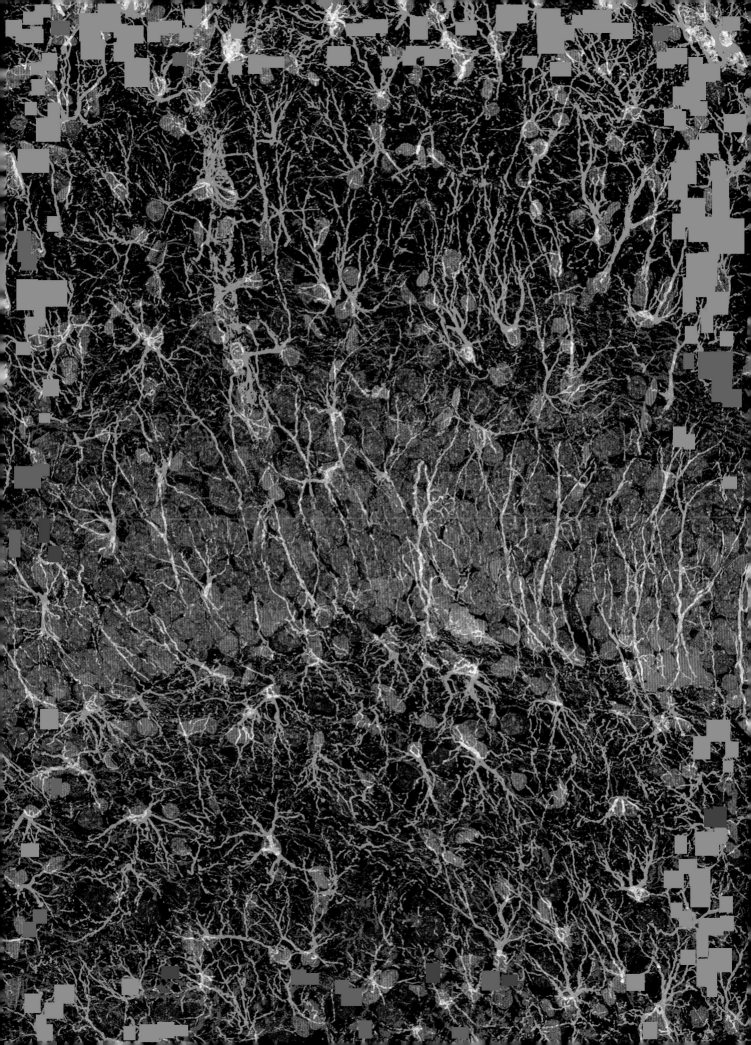

Body bacteria

Did you know there are bacteria all around and inside you?
Some can make you sick, but most are friendly and
don't do any harm. Some you couldn't live without.

Friendly bacteria like
us live in your tummy.
We help you digest
your food.

Skin bacteria

x8,000 E

Your skin is crawling in bacteria.
This is what the bacteria from
skin look like under a very
powerful microscope.

The colors have
been added so
different types of
bacteria stand out.

Some skin bacteria
can cause infections.
Some help KEEP OUT bad
bacteria. And some don't
do anything at all!

Bacteria are SO small that
it's hard to see them with an
ordinary microscope. But you
can grow them until you get a
patch big enough to see...

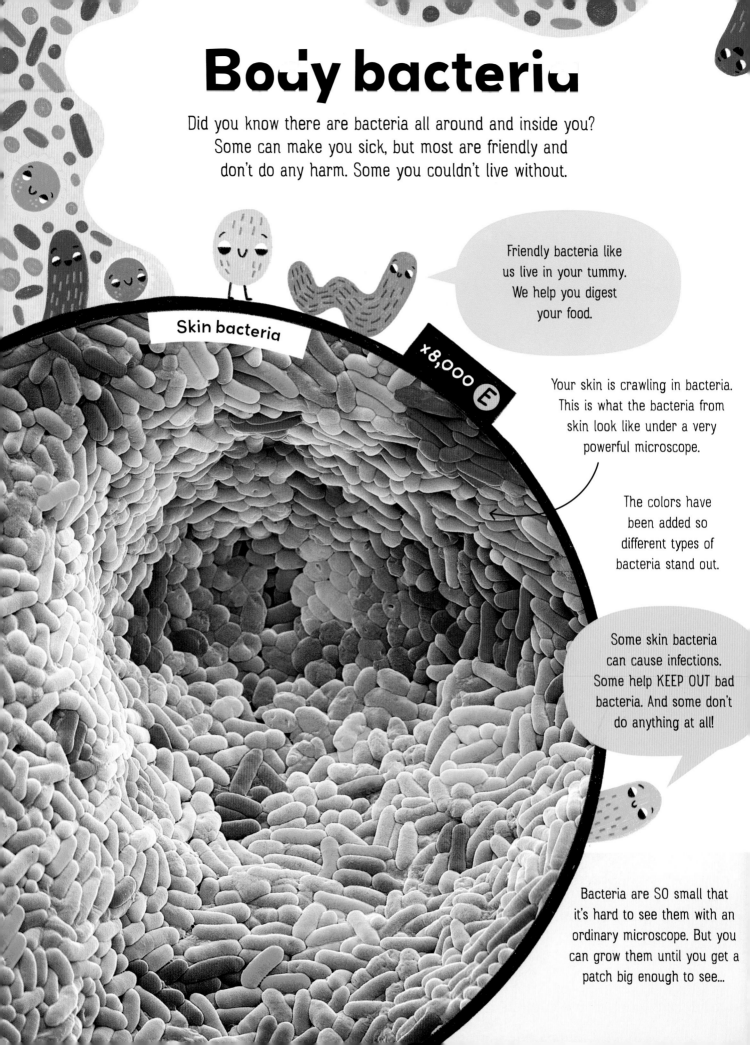

Grow bacteria

You can find petri dishes like these in laboratories all over the world.

YOU WILL NEED

Two plastic petri dishes (you can buy these online) OR plastic tubs with lids, washed out in very hot water first.

1 stock cube (or 1 teaspoon of powdered stock)

1/2 teaspoon of sugar

8.5 oz (250ml) water and a measuring cup

clear tape

1 tbsp powdered gelatin

Gelatin

! This experiment involves boiling water in a pan. Ask a grown-up to help you. Don't touch the bacteria once they're growing.

1 Wash your hands with soapy water. THIS is REALLY important to make sure bacteria don't get into your dishes as you make them.

2 Heat the water in a pan. Add in the stock, sugar and gelatin and stir till they dissolve. Simmer the mixture for half an hour.

! Take care with hot pans.

3 Pour the mixture into a heatproof measuring cup. Pour a thin layer into your two dishes. Put the lids on and leave them to set overnight.

4 Remove the lid from one dish. Press a finger onto the gelatin. Put back the lid and tape it on. Label the dish "unwashed."

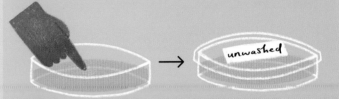
unwashed

5 Now wash your hands thoroughly. Take the lid off the other dish. Press a clean finger onto the gelatin. Put back the lid and tape it on. Label this dish "washed."

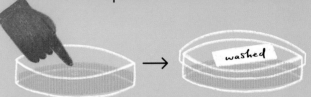
washed

6 Leave the dishes for a few days. You should see some blobs growing on the "unwashed" dish - and nothing on the "washed" dish.

Without removing the lid, look at the blobs with a magnifying glass. Can you see different colors and textures? Those are different TYPES of bacteria.

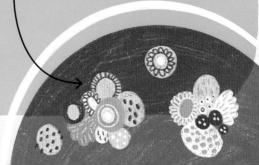

Mould, yeast and bad...

Some types of fungus are bad news for a body, and can cause an infection.
Here's what a few of them look like under a microscope.

Ringworm can give people itchy, red circles on their skin.

x400

Ringworm fungus

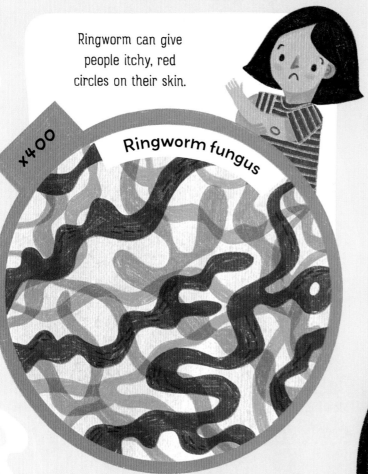

Athlete's foot is a fungal infection that can grow between people's toes and make them sore and itchy.

Athlete's foot fungus

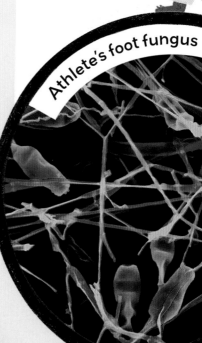

x900

If black fungus gets into your lungs, it can cause serious illness. Most healthy people can fight it off, but it can be dangerous for people who are sick already.

x1,500

Black fungus

All fungi grow by sending out long, thin strands called HYPHAE.

Can you see the hyphae in each of these pictures?

Though some fungi can make people sick, others have SUPERPOWERS that make them great as medicines.

The photo on the right shows a kind of mold called PENICILLIUM. It contains substances that can kill bacteria and is used to make a medicine called penicillin.

Penicillin is used to treat infections including pneumonia and ear infections. Medicines that kill bacteria are known as ANTIBIOTICS.

x1,250 E

Penicillium mold

Over the years, penicillin has saved MILLIONS of lives.

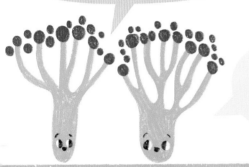

A surprising discovery

In 1928, a British scientist named Alexander Fleming was studying infection-causing bacteria. He was growing them on petri dishes.

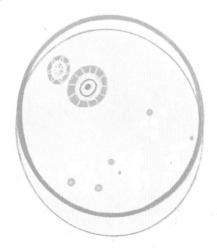

One day Fleming noticed some penicillium mold had grown on one of his dishes by accident. Around it, there were no bacteria.

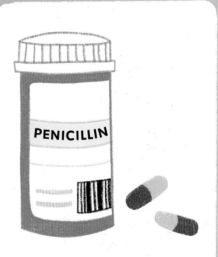

PENICILLIN

He realized penicillium could kill bacteria. That discovery led to the first mass-produced antibiotic: penicillin.

Viruses

Viruses are teeny tiny particles that can get into your body and make you sick. They're so small you need a super powerful microscope to see them.

This is the virus which causes COVID-19. It's part of a group of viruses known as the coronavirus family.

If it gets inside someone's throat or nose, it spreads to their chest and body and makes them sick.

Fighter cells in your blood look out for any virus invaders, like me. If they come across a shape they recognize, they will fight it off.

Corona means "crown" in Latin. Viruses in the coronavirus family have spiky outsides that look a little like crowns.

x150,000 E

Coronavirus

x20,000

Ebola virus

Below is one of the family of influenza viruses, which cause the FLU. Like coronavirus, it gets into someone's body through their throat or nose. The flu makes people feel feverish, achy and sick.

x450,000 E

Flu virus

This is a virus called EBOLA, which can infect people's blood. Someone with Ebola feels very weak and feverish, and can bleed a lot.

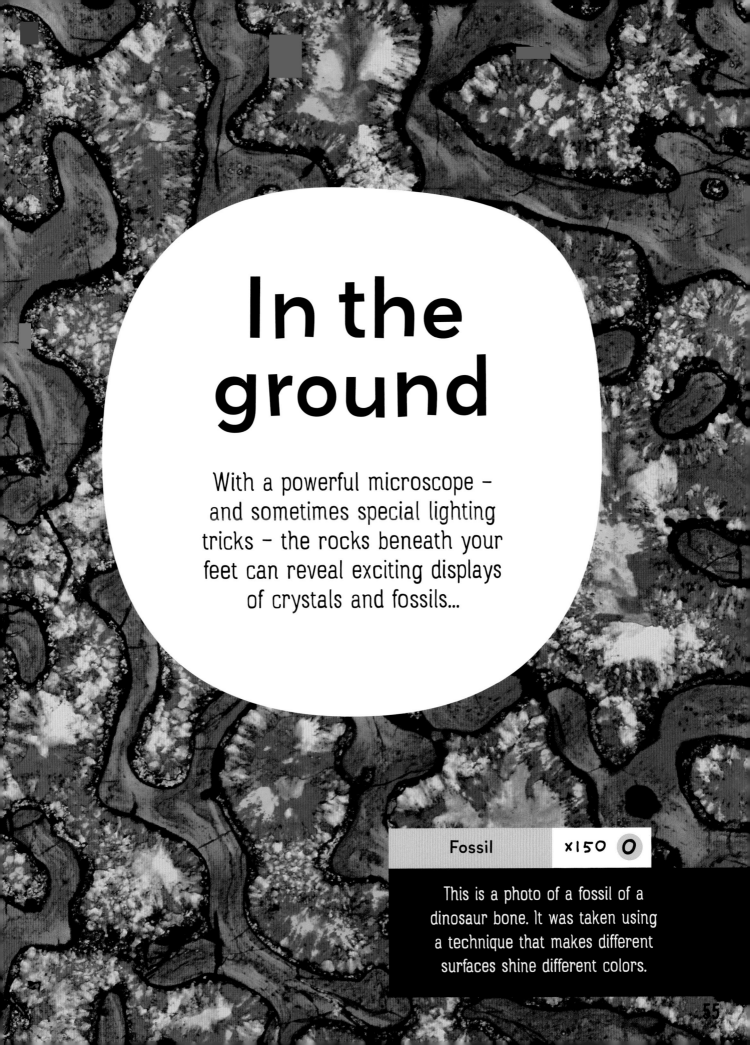

In the ground

With a powerful microscope –
and sometimes special lighting
tricks – the rocks beneath your
feet can reveal exciting displays
of crystals and fossils...

Fossil   ×150 **O**

This is a photo of a fossil of a
dinosaur bone. It was taken using
a technique that makes different
surfaces shine different colors.

Dazzling rocks

Rocks are made from substances called MINERALS. By zooming in on a rock, scientists can figure out which minerals it contains, and where the rock came from.

Scientists often examine rocks under a microscope using special "polarized" light. This makes each texture and surface show up a different color, so it's easier to see what the rock is made of.

The pictures on these pages were made using polarized light.

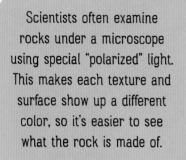

Sandstone

x45

Up close you can see tiny pieces of all sorts of minerals clumped together in this sandstone.

Dunite rock

x40

Sandstone is formed on sea or riverbeds, over thousands and thousands of years. As pieces of rock and sand fall to the seabed, they get crushed together and slowly turn to stone.

This rock contains big chunks of different minerals. It was made when a volcano erupted and super-hot rocks made of different minerals got stuck together.

Crystals

Sometimes, minerals form rocks with especially big, beautiful crystals.

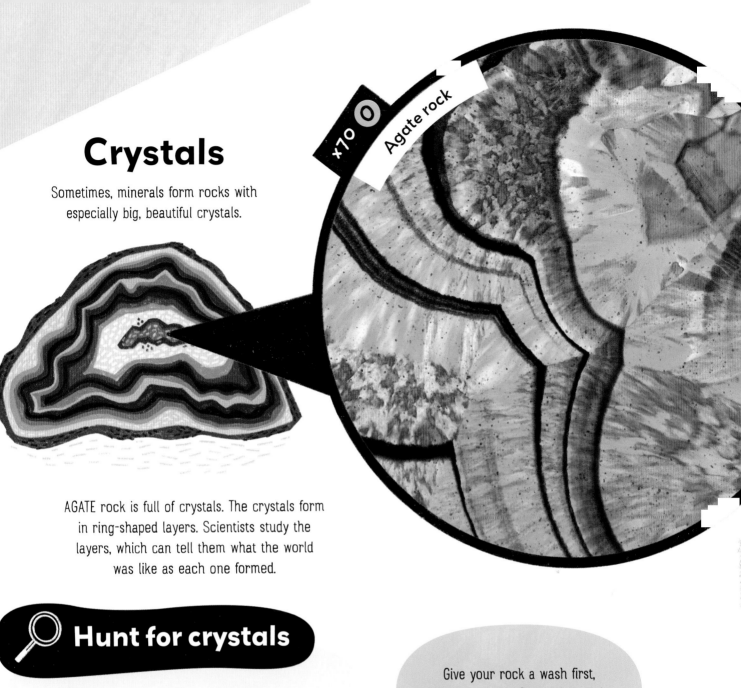

x70

Agate rock

AGATE rock is full of crystals. The crystals form in ring-shaped layers. Scientists study the layers, which can tell them what the world was like as each one formed.

Hunt for crystals

Find some small pebbles and stones to look at through a magnifying glass. Hold them up to the light and turn them from side to side. Can you see any specks that shimmer and shine? Those are CRYSTALS.

Give your rock a wash first, then let it dry. Glints of crystal show up best on DRY rocks.

Tiny fossils

Some rocks, buried deep in the ground or under the sea, contain FOSSILS. Fossils are the rocky remains of plants and animals that lived thousands or even millions of years ago. Some fossils are big enough to see easily, but many are too tiny to spot without a microscope.

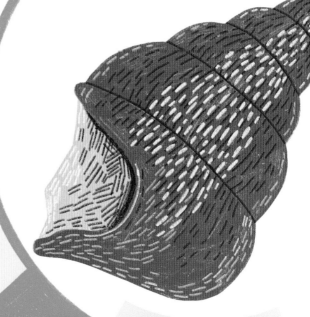

Tiny fossils like the ones on this page are called MICROFOSSILS.

They came from creatures that were no bigger than a grain of sand.

Gastropod fossil
x85

This little seashell is a tiny version of the shells you might see at the beach. Those shells formed recently, but this fossil is very ancient – creatures like this have been around for millions of years.

Foraminiferan fossil
x90

This is one of the most common types of microfossil. It's a tiny sea creature called a foraminiferan. If sea water is polluted, these fossils dissolve. So if scientists find the fossils, it's GOOD NEWS because the sea must be healthy.

Fossils like this one are found in huge numbers in chalk cliffs. It's from a kind of microscopic water creature called a phytoplankton.

x5,500 Ⓔ

Phytoplankton fossil

Sandy treasure

Over years and years, rocks at the coast break down from huge
chunks into small stones, then gradually into tiny grains of sand.
But sand isn't just made of rocks – as you can see if you look up close...

 All sorts in sand

Next time you're at the beach, collect a few
grains of sand. At home, put them on a slide,
and light them from below. What can you find?

You could also look
through a magnifying
glass while you're still
at the beach.

You can use the information here to help you identify things.

Most round-ish grains come from
small STONES. The longer they are
in sand, the smoother they become,
as the rough edges rub away.

Some grains are made of SHELLS, or pieces of shell.
They often have ridges and spirals. Each shell once
had a tiny creature living inside it.

Rough, holey lumps are
probably CORAL. Corals are a type
of animal that live on the seabed.
They form a hard skeleton that gets
washed up and mixed with sand.

Bright, stiff shapes are probably
PLASTIC. Unfortunately there is
a LOT of plastic on beaches and
in the sea, and it lasts a very,
very, very long time.

This is SEA GLASS – little
pieces of glass rubbed
smooth by the sea.

Trouble-shooting

Using a microscope isn't easy, so don't worry if you sometimes struggle to see things. Try the trouble-shooting tips below, and keep on trying!

I can't see anything!

Check the light is on – or, if your microscope has a mirror, that a light is shining brightly on it.

Make sure your sample is right in the middle of the stage, over the light.

Zoom out and search for the sample. When you've spotted it, zoom in slowly, focusing as you go.

Everything just looks blurry.

Look through the eyepiece with one eye, and cover up your other eye. Then adjust the focusing knobs. (If you wear glasses, take them off first.)

The sample won't fit under the lens.

Zoom out! You are too close. Swivel to your SHORTEST lens and try again.

If the sample is just too big, try a magnifying glass instead.

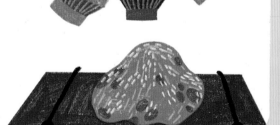

Lots of these things are going wrong and it's very frustrating!

Even experienced scientists find using microscopes difficult sometimes. Take a deep breath and step away. When you're ready to try again, start from the beginning of the instructions.

Up close other ways

Microscopes aren't the only way to zoom in.
Here are some other methods you could try.

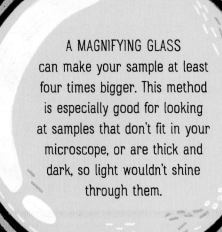

A MAGNIFYING GLASS
can make your sample at least
four times bigger. This method
is especially good for looking
at samples that don't fit in your
microscope, or are thick and
dark, so light wouldn't shine
through them.

FOCUS

x4
x10
x40
x100

Have a look online – go to
usborne.com/Quicklinks and type in the title
of this book. You could try out a virtual
microscope with all sorts of samples, or
download an app that turns a smartphone
or tablet into a handheld magnifier.

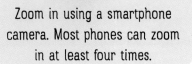

Zoom in using a smartphone
camera. Most phones can zoom
in at least four times.

Glossary

Here is a guide to some of the key words used in this book.
Words in bold have their own entries.

Algae Living things that resemble tiny plants. They live in water and contain **chloroplasts**.

Bacteria Very small, simple living things, made of just one **cell** each.

Cell The basic building block of all living things. Plants, animals, **bacteria** and **fungi** are all made of cells. Most cells contain a **nucleus**.

Chloroplasts Tiny green parts found in most plant **cells**. They make food for the plant, using energy from sunlight.

Coverslip A small, square piece of glass you can put over a **sample** on a **slide**.

Crystal A solid substance that forms in a regular shape, such as salt and sugar. It is often shiny.

Diatoms A type of **algae** made of a single **cell**.

Eyepiece The part of a microscope that you look through. In an **optical microscope**, it contains a **lens**.

Fiber An individual strand of fabric or hair.

Fungi Living things that grow like plants but, unlike plants, can't make their own food. Includes mushrooms and **molds**.

Lens A curved piece of glass used to change how big things look. A magnifying glass is one big lens. An **optical microscope** has several small lenses that work together.

Magnification How much an image is zoomed in by, for example x100 means 100 times larger than life. The bigger the magnification, the more detail you can see.

Microorganism A term for living things that are generally too small to see with the naked eye.

Microscope A device for looking at things that are too small to see clearly with the naked eye.

> **Electron microscope** A device that uses a tiny stream of electrons to create a magnified image. Usually found in science labs and very powerful.

> **Optical microscope** A device that uses light and glass **lenses** to create a magnified image. Most home microscopes are optical microscopes.

Mold A type of **fungus** often found growing on rotting food.

Nucleus A part in the middle of most **cells** that controls what the cell does.

Pollen Powder in flowers that is spread by insects or the wind, and helps the plant reproduce.

Sample The thing that you are viewing with your **microscope**.

Slide A rectangular piece of glass on which you can put a **sample**, before viewing with an **optical microscope**.

Spores Tiny, single **cells** that **fungi** use to reproduce.

Stage The part at the bottom of an **optical microscope** where you place the **sample**.

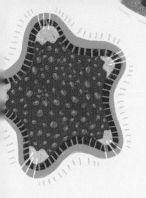
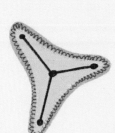
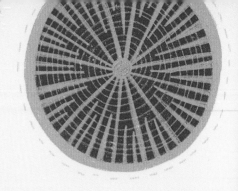

Index

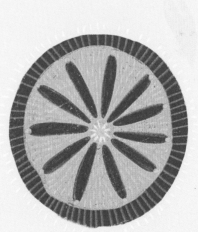

Turn to the pages listed to find out lots about each of these things!

Photo credits

Cover: Syrup crystals, optical microscope photo © Microckscopica / Science Photo Library (SPL); Mushroom gills, optical microscope photo © Frank Fox / SPL; Leaf cells, optical microscope photo © John Durham / SPL; Butterfly wing scales, optical microscope photo © Frank Fox / SPL. Pages 2-3: Butterfly wing scales, electron microscope photo © Alex Hyde / SPL. Pages 4-5: Tardigrade (*Hypsibius dujardini*), microscopic photograph © blickwinkel / Hecker / Sauer / Alamy Stock Photo; Ammophilia, leaf, optical microscope photo © M.I. Walker / Science Source / SPL; Penicillium mold, optical microscope photo © Dr Keith Wheeler / SPL. Pages 6-7: Venus flytrap pollen grains, electron microscope photo © Kevin Mackenzie, University of Aberdeen / SPL; Male flea, optical microscope photo © Steve Gschmeissner / SPL; Human flea, electron microscope photo © Steve Gschmeissner / SPL. Pages 8-9: Cotton fibers, optical microscope photo © Panther Media GmbH / Alamy Stock Photo. Pages 10-11: Swimsuit material, electron microscope photo © Eye of Science / SPL. Pages 12-13: Paper, electron microscope photo © Susumu Nishinaga / SPL. Pages 14-15: Cork cells, Hooke's Micrographia © Omikron / SPL; Euro banknote details, optical microscope photo © Marek Mis / SPL. Pages 16-17: Household dust, electron microscope photo © Power and Syred / SPL; Synthetic sponge, electron microscope photo © Power and Syred / SPL. Pages 18-19: Silicon chip, electron microscope photo © Eye Of Science / SPL; Syrup crystals, optical microscope photo © Microckscopica / SPL. Pages 20-21: Chicken eggshell cross section, electron microscope photo © Dennis Kunkel Microscopy / SPL; Chicken eggshell surface, electron microscope photo © Dennis Kunkel Microscopy / SPL. Pages 22-23: Sugar crystals, electron microscope photo © Susumu Nishinaga / SPL. Pages 24-25: Mushroom gills, optical microscope photo © Frank Fox / SPL; Stilton cheese, electron microscope photo © Dr Jeremy Burgess / SPL. Pages 26-27 Flame lily pollen, electron microscope photo © Steve Gschmeissner / SPL. Pages 28-29: Onion epidermis, optical microscope photo © Peter Hermes Furian / Alamy Stock Photo. Pages 30-31: Gorse petal surface, electron microscope photo © Peter Bond, EM Centre, University Of Plymouth / SPL; Foxglove petal, electron microscope photo © Eye Of Science / SPL; Pollen, electron microscope photo © Steve Gschmeissner / SPL. Pages 32-33: Orchid petal, electron microscope photo © Steve Gschmeissner / SPL; Poppy root, optical microscope photo © Hervé Conge, ISM / SPL. Pages 36-37: Trichomes, electron microscope photo © Steve Gschmeissner / SPL; Moth wing scales, electron microscope photo © Steve Gschmeissner / SPL. Pages 38-39: Water bear, electron microscope photo © Eye Of Science / SPL; Black aphid feeding on sap, electron microscope photo © Clouds Hill Imaging Ltd / SPL. Pages 40-41: Butterfly wing scales, electron microscope photo © Alex Hyde / SPL. Pages 42-43: Gecko foot, electron microscope photo © Power And Syred / SPL; Butterfly eye and proboscis, electron microscope photo © Dennis Kunkel Microscopy / SPL; Spiny dogfish skin, electron microscope photo © Eye Of Science / SPL. Pages 44-45: Penguin feather, electron microscope photo © Steve Gschmeissner / SPL; Bacteria, electron microscope photo © Steve Gschmeissner / SPL. Pages 46-47: Skin section, optical microscope photo © Alfred Pasieka / SPL; Mouth skin cells, optical microscope photo © Hervé Conge - ISM / SPL. Pages 48-49: Hippocampus brain tissue, optical microscope photo © Thomas Deerinck, NCMIR / SPL. Pages 50-51: Skin bacteria, electron microscope photo © Steve Gschmeissner / SPL. Pages 52-53: Athlete's foot fungus, electron microscope photo © Dennis Kunkel Microscopy / SPL; Penicillium spores, electron microscope photo © Eye Of Science / SPL. Pages 54-55: Covid-19 coronavirus particles, electron microscope photo © NIAID-RML / National Institutes Of Health / SPL; Influenza virus, electron microscope photo © Cavallini James / BSIP / SPL; Dinosaur fossil, optical microscope photo © Microckscopica / SPL. Pages 56-57: Dunite, optical microscope photo © Microckscopica / SPL; Agate from Brazil, optical microscope photo © Microckscopica / SPL. Pages 58-59: Calcareous phytoplankton, electron microscope photo © Steve Gschmeissner / SPL.

Series editor: Rosie Dickins

Series designer: Stephen Moncrieff

With additional content by Eddie Reynolds
Photographic manipulation by John Russell

First published in 2022 by Usborne Publishing Ltd., Usborne House, 83-85 Saffron Hill, London, EC1N 8RT, United Kingdom, usborne.com Copyright © 2022 Usborne Publishing Ltd. The name Usborne and the Balloon logos are trade marks of Usborne Publishing Ltd. All rights reserved. No part of this publication may be reproduced, stored in any retrieval system, or transmitted in any form or by any means, without the prior permission of the publisher. Printed in UAE.
First published in America in 2024.